WITHDRAWN

In Every War But One

IN EVERY WAR
BUT ONE

BY EUGENE KINKEAD

W · W · NORTON & COMPANY · INC ·

NEW YORK

Library of Congress Catalog Card No. 58-11107

PRINTED IN THE UNITED STATES OF AMERICA
FOR THE PUBLISHERS BY VAIL-BALLOU PRESS

TO
DUNCAN
AND
ALL OTHER
FUTURE U. S. SERVICEMEN

Contents

Preface

It is a truism that no nation can expect to survive unless it knows the nature of its enemy and unless it maintains the moral tone as well as the armed strength necessary to defend itself against him. We Americans have had available to us for a quarter of a century a long stream of testimonials, starting at least as early as the Moscow trials of 1936, which reveal to us the new methods that Communists use to manipulate the minds of human beings—a technique called variously indoctrination, brainwashing, thought reform, and other things. Call it what you will, it is the total psychological weapon by means of which, equally with its sputniks and armed might, Soviet Russia firmly expects to conquer the rest of the world.

But it is human nature not to feel the full strength of a threat until one has actually measured oneself against it. It is also part of American buoyancy to discount subtle and devious evil. The Korean War was the first time that America as a whole met its enemy—totalitarian Communism. For it was not just our young soldiers who faced the

9

antagonist, but more importantly the entire cultural pattern which produced these young soldiers. When our contact with the enemy was on the field of battle, we fared better than when we met him on a personal basis, face to face, mind to mind, culture to culture, in his prison camps. In a high percentage of these personal meetings, we not only did not hold our own, but we failed signally. Many captives fell victims to Communist indoctrination.

One result of our failure was a five-year study made by the Army to determine exactly what had happened to its men in the Korean prison camps, and why it had happened. Parts of the Army investigation have been touched on now and again in newspapers and magazines; but a complete report of the study has never been published, nor have its massive data been interpreted for the country at large. The study lies buried in bits and pieces around the military landscape—in the voluminous and now retired prisoner files, in official briefings, in reports before various committees, in diverse memoranda gathering dust these days in forgotten cabinets . . . and in the minds of the men who composed its now disbanded research groups and who are presently scattered in new assignments across the country and the world.

Because I felt it was important that the story of the Army investigation should be brought to the attention of as many Americans as possible, I wrote, first, the Reporter At Large article, "The Study of Something New In History," which was published in *The New Yorker* magazine of October 26,

1957; and, secondly, I expanded that article into this book. The story, I felt, was important for two reasons. First, it was obviously a significant piece of American history which otherwise would be known entirely to only a handful of uniformed specialists. The second reason, and to my mind the more important, was—it sets a haunting and inescapable challenge to every American.

I first asked the Army for permission to report its investigation in early 1954, while the investigation was still in progress. A wait of more than a year ensued before permission was finally granted. No writer, however, could have wanted greater cooperation once the bars were down. In the almost three years that it has taken me to assemble and analyze the material, the Army offered unstinted aid, and in due course what I wrote was approved by the Department of Defense. The fact that the Army, once it decided to go ahead, was not only willing, but eager, to devote a great deal of time to a citizen journalist who had much to learn as he went along is, I believe, an inspiriting sign of the vigor of our democracy. The Army was not only willing to admit its share in the shortcomings that the investigation revealed; it pointed them out to me.

Equally helpful in this long-drawn-out venture was the firm support of the editor of The New Yorker, William Shawn, whose editorial skill and judgment did much to shape the form of the magazine article. The response to this article was heartening and heady. From every part of the country, people wrote in, showing they were studying, contemplating, and discussing the study's obvious messages and the responses that these had aroused in them.

I felt that presenting the mass of technical material in orthodox expository form would merely bury the statistics under their own weight and beget a handful of dry generalities. Accordingly, I decided to assemble the data in an interview pattern which would, I hoped, maintain the quality of human poignancy and lend cumulative narrative strength.

To know is to be forewarned. The facts that follow will, I trust, provide some aid—physical, mental, and spiritual—against the menace of Communism not only to Americans, but to all those people everywhere who love and want the way of freedom.

Eugene Kinkead

Chappaqua, New York

In Every War But One

Korean War Chronology

1950

June	War starts with Communist North Korean invasion of South Korea. Seoul falls.
July	U. S. ground troops, part of U.N. forces, first engage North Korean enemy.
August	U.N. units, although nearly driven into sea, hold Pusan beachhead.
September–October	U.N. counterattack virtually wipes out North Korean army. U.N. troops advance on Manchurian border.
November	Chinese Communists enter war. U.N. forces soon pushed back to middle of peninsula.

1951

January	First permanent Communist prisoner-of-war camps set up on Yalu River.
March	Prisoner indoctrination starts.
July	Truce negotiations start.

1952

	Military stalemate. Fighting seesaws along old demarcation line. Truce negotiations continue.

1953

April–May	*Operation Little Switch.* 149 sick and wounded American prisoners returned.
July	Armistice signed.
August–September	*Operation Big Switch.* 3,629 American prisoners repatriated.

I

The Exceptional War

Sad and Singular Record of Korean Prisoners—Promulgation of
Code of Conduct—Lack of Public Information on Prisoner
Conditions—Start of This Report

In every war but one that the United States has fought, the
conduct of those of its servicemen who were captured and
held in enemy prison camps presented no unforeseen problems to the armed forces and gave rise to no particular concern in the country as a whole. In some of those camps—
British camps during the Revolution, both Union and Con-
federate camps during the Civil War, and Japanese camps
during the Second World War—our men were grievously
treated, and fell victims to starvation and disease. In none
of them, though, was there a wholesale breakdown of morale
or wholesale collaboration with the captors. Moreover, whatever the rigors of the camps, in every war but one a respec-
table number of prisoners managed, through ingenuity,
daring, and plain good luck, to escape. That one war was
the Korean War.

15

As everybody knows, twenty-one of the Americans captured during the Korean war decided to remain with the enemy—the only time in history that American captives have chosen not to return home because they preferred the enemy's form of government to our own. The action, of course, was all the more astonishing because the enemy's form of government was so unlike our own. What was even more shocking—for, after all, the twenty-one men could be regarded as ideological cranks—was the fact that almost one out of every three American prisoners in Korea was guilty of some sort of collaboration with the enemy. The degree of collaboration ranged from such serious offenses as writing anti-American propaganda and informing on their comrades to the relatively innocuous offense of broadcasting Christmas greetings home and thereby putting the Communists in a favorable light, because such broadcasts had to include a report of good treatment at their hands. Then, when the war ended and the prisoners began to return, it became clear that some of them had behaved brutally to their fellow-prisoners; and for a time the newspapers carried reports of grisly incidents in the prison camps, including the murder of Americans by other Americans. (The most notorious offender, perhaps, was Sergeant James C. Gallagher, who was convicted by a court-martial of killing two seriously ill fellow prisoners by throwing them out into the snow.) Furthermore, during the entire Korean conflict not one of our men escaped from a permanent enemy prison camp and successfully made his way back to our lines. And, finally, to mention something that might not on the face of it seem to point to any moral or disciplinary weakness among the prisoners, 38 per cent of them—2,730 out of a total of 7,190—died in captivity. This is a higher prisoner death rate than that of any of our previous wars, including the Revolution, in which it is estimated that about 33 per cent of the prisoners died.

All in all, sinister and regrettable things happened in the prison camps of North Korea. The public has been inclined to attribute them solely to the cruelty of the Communists, particularly to the mysterious technique known as "brainwashing." The officials involved, however— in the Defense Department—and especially in the Army, which, because of the nature of the operations in Korea, supplied more than 90 per cent of the American service men who fought there—could not accept an explanation as simple as that. For one thing, there was evidence that the high death rate was not due primarily to Communist maltreatment—that it could be accounted for largely by the ignorance or the callousness of the prisoners themselves. For another, the prisoners, as far as Army psychiatrists have been able to discover, were not subjected to anything that could properly be called brainwashing. Indeed, the Communist treatment of prisoners, while it came nowhere near fulfilling the requirements of the Geneva Convention, rarely involved outright cruelty, being instead a highly novel blend of leniency and pressure. If our prisoners had behaved strangely, the explanation was bound to be a good deal more complex than brainwashing and simple brutality. The explanation, the Army found, is indeed complex; it is also frightening or challenging, depending on a person's outlook.

There seem to be no easy generalities that can be made about why these things occurred, simply because the explanation for their occurrence cannot be the same for every man. Instead, the roots of the explanation go deep into diverse aspects of our culture—home training of children, education, physical fitness, religious adherence, and the privilege of existing under the highest standard of living in the world. In the light of what happened in Korea, all of these facets of American life might profitably be re-examined by our leaders in government, education, and religion.

That some of our prisoners were behaving strangely became evident surprisingly early in the hostilities—at 11:55 A.M., Greenwich time, on July 9, 1950, to be precise, or only four days after our ground forces had first engaged the enemy in Korea. At that time an American Army officer of the 24th Infantry Division, taken prisoner some forty-eight hours before, made a nine-hundred-word broadcast in the enemy's behalf over the Seoul radio. Purportedly speaking for all American soldiers, this man said, among other things, "We did not know at all the cause of the war and the real state of affairs, and were compelled to fight against the people of Korea. It was really most generous of the Democratic People's Republic of Korea to forgive us and give kind consideration for our health, for food, clothing, and habitation." Service authorities were dumfounded. Parts of the statement, of course, were actually treasonable. But a tape recording had been made of the broadcast and there was no mistaking the officer's voice. Within a few weeks, many statements of this sort were picked up by American listening posts in the Far East.

Accordingly, the Army soon began collecting data for a formal study of the behavior of its men taken prisoners of war in Korea. This tremendous and detailed study, of a scope and complexity never before attempted by the armed services of this country, made an effort to obtain all pertinent facts about the background and prison experiences of every American soldier taken captive in the Korean conflict who was returned to us. Almost four thousand case histories were put together and carefully examined. The study began in the latter part of the summer of 1950, and ended on July 29, 1955, five years later, two years and two days after the signing of the armistice at Panmunjom. Its broad aims were to evaluate both the Communist treatment of Army prisoners, and the various problems that this treatment raised, including its military, medical, psychiatric, propagandistic, and legal effects. In addition, the study noted the possible hazard to national security posed by GI's who had undergone prolonged ideological pressure at the hands of the Reds and had been since discharged from the service.

By far, the most important result thus far to come out of the Army study was the promulgation on August 17, 1955, by President Eisenhower of the new Code of Conduct for Members of the Armed Forces of the United States. The significance of this document has by no means yet been fully appreciated by the people of this country.

The Code of Conduct was (like the events in Korea that inspired it) completely unprecedented. Never before had a President found it necessary to clarify or restate the principles of conduct for our military personnel, which had heretofore always been prescribed in regular training manuals. The fact that it was necessary to spell out what had always been taken for granted by Americans as constituting the unquestioned duties and obligations of our fighting men showed how greatly the Korean War differed from the seven previous major wars that this nation had fought.

The Code makes its points clearly in six simple articles.

I

I am an American fighting man. I serve in the forces which guard my country and our way of life. I am prepared to give my life in their defense.

II

I will never surrender of my own free will. If in command I will never surrender my men while they have the means to resist.

III

If I am captured I will continue to resist by all means available. I will make every effort to escape and aid others to escape. I will accept neither parole nor special favors from the enemy.

IV

If I become a prisoner of war I will keep faith with my fellow prisoners. I will give no information or take part in any action which might be harmful to my comrades. If I am senior, I will take command. If not, I will obey the lawful orders of those appointed over me and will back them up in every way.

V

When questioned, should I become a prisoner of war, I am bound to give only name, rank, service number, and date of birth. I will evade answering further questions to the utmost of my ability. I will make no oral or written statements disloyal to my country and its allies or harmful to their cause.

VI

I will never forget that I am an American fighting man, responsible for my actions, and dedicated to the principles which made my country free. I will trust in my God and in the United States of America.

The promulgation of this set of principles means that the government of the United States, because of what happened in the prison camps of the Korean War, is prepared to try to mold a new set of fundamental attitudes in its citizens in the armed forces, with a view to helping them, and the nation itself, survive any future war.

Before the appearance of the Code, the data offered the public on what it was like to have been a prisoner of war in Korea had been fragmentary and confusing. Often the information was highly colored, and most of it was unofficial. The Marine Corps had published the findings of a 1953 investigation into the conduct of one of its fliers, Colonel Frank H. Schwable, who had been charged with collaboration, together with some paragraphs of comment.

From the released text, however, it was apparent that Schwable's was a special case in that he had been held incommunicado from all other prisoners. After the end of the war, more than a dozen trials of Army personnel accused of misconduct as prisoners had been reported in the newspapers; but the accounts of the trials were slanted, consciously or unconsciously by the feelings of the reporters who had covered them, and so were often contradictory.

In addition, a few quasi-official documents had been published, such as General Dean's memories of his imprisonment. But again, General Dean's experiences could not be called typical, inasmuch as he had also received special treatment, being kept apart from other captives. Finally, there had been a number of interviews in newspapers and magazines with individuals who had undergone imprisonment at Communist hands. Very few of the statements that these people made were officially authorized or officially assessed. What was dramatic in their recollections naturally tended to assume major importance or was emphasized in the articles and newspapers. The articles themselves were often conflicting: some mentioned the overpowering effects of physical torture, others doggedly successful resistance to it; some stressed widespread American treachery, and others widespread American heroism. The Communists' use of indoctrination and interrogation was mentioned in all this popularly published material. These were obviously important techniques in the enemy handling of prisoners, but any description of them or the results they produced usually varied with each account. These techniques were lumped by the man in the street under the general term of "brainwashing," but his concept of brainwashing was especially hazy.

So much for material that was published before the appearance of the Code of Conduct. The day that the Code was promulgated the committee that had recommended it issued an account of the deliberations that had led to the decision in the form of a fourteen-thousand-word report entitled *POW—The Fight Continues After The Battle.* The report was a rationale of the committee's thinking on the many complex problems it had considered, and included a lengthy historical survey of the changing status of prisoners, a judgment on the views presented to the committee, and a reaffirmation, based on the pronouncements of the Code, that America supported the principle of morality against the principle of expediency. It concluded with the sentence, "The Korean story must never be permitted to happen again." The wording of the rather hurriedly written report was dry and necessarily somewhat general. It did, however, provide the first official assessment —although perforce a very sketchy one because of the summary nature of the document—of what it had been like to be a prisoner of war in Korea. The report has, unfortunately, been read far less widely than the information in it deserves.

Early in 1955, after a year of waiting, I finally acquired the Army's cooperation to investigate and report on its prisoner study. It was my wish to correct the incomplete and contradictory picture that had grown up in the public mind of what it had been like to be a prisoner in Korea. I had become interested in this problem soon after the cease-fire at Panmunjom. As a Pacific area war correspondent almost ten years before, in World War II, I had been impressed by the general toughness, the independence, and the loyalty of the American fighting man. Accordingly, I was puzzled by what had happened in Korea.

Early in 1954 I wrote Earl Johnson, who was then Under Secretary of the Army, requesting the official cooperation of his service in getting the facts, as far as the Army might have been able to obtain them, on several of the more notable instances of prisoner misconduct in Korea. I wanted to analyze these psychologically in a magazine article whose conclusions might or might not be palatable to Americans because I felt that Americans should be thinking about Communist psychology, its aims, and its methods.

My partner in the proposed project was Professor John Dollard, of Yale University's Institute of Human Relations, an old friend with special qualifications for what we had in mind. A well-known sociologist, Dollard had been a Special Assistant to the Secretary of War during World War II, doing research on fear in battle, and on other emotional aspects of military problems. We planned to handle the assignment as a journalist-psychologist team.

Johnson forwarded my letter with a favorable recommendation to the proper authorities, from whom I heard in due course. In its reply the Army asked that I postpone my request for a year, because it was at that point itself studying the matters mentioned in my letter. Until the Army reached some conclusions on these problems, there could naturally be no official discussion of any aspects of its study.

I renewed my application after a year. It was granted, and Dollard and I went to Washington, where we met members of the Army study group. These men made two very significant changes in our project. First, they told us, our sights were too narrow. The Army study was much broader than the psychological consideration of a handful of incidents; it embraced everything that could be learned about Army prisoners in Korea, and any reporting of the study should consequently be along these broader lines.

Second, the officials cut the ground out from under Dollard's place in our plans. They said that the problem of Korean prisoner behavior was not one to be tackled from the viewpoint of psychiatry or psychology alone; and in cases in which these things were important, the Army psychologists and psychiatrists were the ones to explain the study's conclusions. Therefore, Dollard, to the regret of us both, felt that he must withdraw.

For the next three years, looking into and writing about the Army study was my main occupation. After I had acquired sufficient background through a number of weeks of research and briefings, the office of the Army's Chief of Information arranged a schedule of appointments for me with individuals involved in the service's prisoner study, and my interviewing began.

25

II

Why They Collaborated

Introductory Views of Honorable Hugh M. Milton II, Assistant
Secretary of the Army—Indoctrination versus Brainwashing—
Extent of Collaboration

When the men with whom I talked in Washington discussed the conclusions they had come to in the course of the
Army study, they often seemed to be stating the obvious,
repeating platitudes, or talking without saying anything at
all. After a while, however, I realized that they were saying
a great deal, and that on questions of human behavior much
that sounded old was so old that it was new again. The
psychological, philosophical, and moral problems that these
men were dealing with were so simple and basic that the
conclusions they reached after considerable thought about
a stupendous collection of data were also, necessarily, simple and basic. President Eisenhower's six-point code repre-
sented a distillation of their conclusions. We had finished
a war with an enemy who had fought not only on the battle-

26

field but also in prison camps, by manipulating the minds of the prisoners; and our government and the Army had come to see that our servicemen not only had to be trained how to fight physically—they had to know how to fight back mentally and morally as well.

My first appointment was with Mr. Hugh M. Milton II, Assistant Secretary of the Army for Manpower and Reserve Forces. He was the official at the secretarial level directly in charge of the Army's prisoner-of-war study, and later became a member of the Defense Department Committee that advocated the Code. Mr. Milton, I had been told by the Army Information Office spokesman who arranged my schedule, would give me a general idea of some of the more important discoveries the Army had made in its study. He would then pass me along to other officials of the department who would be able to fill in the pertinent details.

Milton is a tall, dark, friendly Kentuckian, sixty-one years old, who, before he entered the government, was president of the New Mexico Agricultural and Mechanical College. He began our talk by saying that in the war in Korea the American Army had been engaged, for the first time in the 180 years since it was founded, with an enemy to whom combat tactics meant not merely fighting on the battle-field, but handling prisoners as well. Though the idea of extending combat into the prison camps is in direct contravention of all the rules of warfare which are embodied in the Geneva Convention, Milton said, the Communists did it, and did it continuously.

27

The Army had its first intimation of this new concept of fighting early in the hostilities, on July 9, 1950, with the speech mentioned earlier which the 24th Infantry Division officer broadcast from Seoul. In this broadcast, the officer had also said, Milton told me, "Dear friends, we, all prisoners, solidly appeal to you as follows: the armed intervention in Korean internal affairs is quite a barbaristic, aggressive action to protect the benefit of the capital monopolists of the U.S.A. Let us fight for right against wrong, bravely opposing to be mobilized into such a war against Russia."

"The incident was unthinkable," Milton said. "Such conduct is, of course, in absolute violation of the Army training rule that states specifically that no aid or comfort of any sort be given to the enemy, that a soldier when captured is still a soldier of his country, from whom loyalty is still required. This broadcast, and others like it that followed shortly, soon alerted us to the fact that in Korea we were indeed fighting a new and different kind of war."

It at once became plain, moreover, that radio messages were only one phase of the Communists' illegal exploitation of prisoners. In addition to broadcasts, which continued for the duration of the war, the enemy soon began returning small groups of captives, who had been subjected to special indoctrination and were loaded with propaganda leaflets, to our front lines, trying by this means to influence our troops to desert to Communism. Some of the families of prisoners turned over to the Army letters they had received that sounded wholly unlike the men who had written

28

them. These letters all harped on a single theme—the hope
for a quick restoration of international peace—though the
writers of the letters, as well as the recipients, presumably
knew full well that the Communists were completely responsible for destroying that peace in the first place. And
within a few months after the conflict began, articles by
captive GI's praising life under Communism began to appear in the Moscow-dominated press in India, North Africa,
Indonesia, and elsewhere. All these acts were far from being
pointless, disconnected moves. They were clearly part of a
well-thought-out Communist design to use our prisoners as
a means of attacking us on fronts other than the actual
fighting line by inducing them to declare pro-Communist
convictions both to American soldiers who had not been
captured, and to their parents at home, and to parade these
convictions before the diplomats and nationals of non-
Communist countries.

"Let me illustrate how the technique worked on the
diplomatic front," Milton said. "The Communists' method
was to give the widest possible circulation to favorable
statements made about them by our prisoners. These were
generally to the effect that the Communists were nice
fellows and Americans were aggressive warmongers. At least
one of these published statements was reprinted as a United
Nations Security Council document by the Soviets in 1950,
when Jacob Malik was chairman of that body. This was
done obviously with the idea of harassing the United States
diplomatic program, which was then actively maintaining

that the Communists had started the war, and with the further objective, of course, of influencing any U. N. delegation that could be influenced to side in this matter with the Communists.

"Very much a part of the same total strategy, but probably a more important part, was the dissemination of these pro-Communist statements, broadcast and published in many languages, to neutral countries and to overpopulated and backward areas of the globe where the Communists were trying desperately to attract converts to their cause. You can see how difficult it was for our government to refute such lies to people in the hinterlands of Asia, for instance, when the statements were accompanied by the names and often, when published in newspapers, by the pictures of actual American soldiers. It is hard to say how much democracy suffered in areas like this because of such statements by our men. Unquestionably they helped the enemy. Since they were made mostly by Army personnel, the Army took note of them in its study. It also noted that the use to which these statements were put seemed clearly just another part of the Communists' worldwide propaganda plan."

This sort of thing—American troops collaborating in such large numbers, and apparently so casually—was incredible, Milton went on, and yet it was happening. The puzzled Army resolved that if those men ever got back, every one of them would be questioned about his experiences after capture and about the Communist techniques of handling prisoners. "The resulting Army study was the first in history to go into the background and prison experiences of every American soldier captured during a war," Milton said. "Some of my colleagues will be telling you about its mechanics and its conclusions, but I will say this much: After it was completed, we knew a great deal more than we had known about Communist methods and about the way our men reacted to them. No limit was set on the length of the men's answers to our questions, and all told, they must run to several million pages. The data are extremely valuable, and the study may be unique in the world. From it we learned, among other things, how the Communists managed to persuade most of the captives to attend classes where Communist theory was drummed into them. The Army calls this 'indoctrination.' The alternative term, 'brainwashing,' has become a catch phrase, used for so many things that it no longer has any precise meaning— and, as you'll find out, a precise meaning is necessary in this case."

One of the results of the Army study has been to make it possible to clearly define the term, *indoctrination*. Indoctrination was defined for me later in the course of my investigation by one of the study's chief psychiatrists. "Unfortunately, the distinction between brainwashing and indoctrination is far from clear to the average American," this doctor said. "The Army defines indoctrination as an effort to change a man's viewpoint while he is still a thinking individual by regulating his thoughts and actions. This falls far short of the effect produced upon some defendants seen in Communist courts, defendants who had obviously been completely broken, and had ceased to be thinking individuals. I am afraid that the general conception has been that Communist techniques of manipulating human beings are so persuasive, so completely irresistible, that no prisoner can keep his integrity in the face of them—and, by analogy, that no people, including ours, can stand against such an enemy. This is what distresses me so much about the popular and improper use of a word like brainwashing. In our society, when we face a phenomenon that we do not completely understand, we are apt to give it a name that indicates there is something magical, something beyond the reach of man's powers of comprehension, about it. 'My goodness,' we say in effect by giving a process which has many aspects this particular name, 'look at this! You can remove a man's brain and wash out what's in it, and wash into it whatever you want, the way you manage tape on a tape recorder!' The terrible implications of the term itself undermine the will of some people to resist. This is foolish. If only we can get to the point where we really understand indoctrination, we will have taken a long step forward in defeating it.

"Let me give you an illustration of how knowledge of any phenomenon invariably helps, no matter what we're facing. In the days just after the Chinese intervened in the Korean War, their bugle calls had a tendency to panic our troops. Uncertainty prevailed whenever one was heard. What did it mean—a flanking movement, a retreat, an attack? Often a bugle was blown in the dead of night, around the time when attacks were generally launched. But sometimes no attack came. Some of these calls apparently meant nothing; but not understanding them put our men at a psychological disadvantage that was a real handicap to them in combat. One of our generals, hearing about this, got troops returning from the front lines to describe the various calls, even the ones that seemed to mean nothing. By correlating them with what had actually happened in the line each time a call was heard, he was able before long to decode them. They proved to be an easily recognizable set of signals, and once the information as to what each one stood for was disseminated among our troops, the calls completely lost their menace and even became a help to us in combat. So it could be with an understanding of indoctrination. If we could do away with all the awe and mystery about it, and simply study its methods, we would realize, I am convinced, that it can be dealt with by very simple countermeasures that demand only firmness of application."

That twin of indoctrination, interrogation, was also discussed by Mr. Milton during our interview. It has, unsurprisingly, in Communist hands an application quite different from its usual one.

"We naturally also learned a good deal about the special Communist uses of interrogation during our study," Mr. Milton said. "Interrogation is a legitimate method of trying to elicit military information, of course; but the Communists used it not so much for this as to produce a state of mind that would be vulnerable to indoctrination—in other words, to change a man's political views and obtain his collaboration. The Communists rarely used physical torture—you'll hear more about that as you go along—and the Army has not found a single verifiable case in which they used it for the specific purpose of forcing a man to collaborate or to accept their convictions. The enemy did, however, apply many forms of mental pressure and physical hardship—withholding food, medicine, and hospital care, for example—and, of course, using such techniques to change political views is not only illegal by all the recognized codes for prisoner handling, but is completely contrary to the basic tenets of humanity. But say what we will, condemn it as we like, it is a cold, hard fact of Communist practice. It may sound trite, but if America is going to survive, Americans must learn to cope with this practice."

I asked Milton if he could estimate the percentage of prisoners who had collaborated. He replied, "If we use as a standard the committing of some perhaps understandable act of 'technical' collaboration, such as broadcasting Christmas greetings to relatives at home, the percentage might run as high as thirty per cent. One man in every seven, or more than thirteen per cent, was guilty of serious collaboration—writing disloyal tracts, say, or agreeing to spy or organize for the Communists after the war." He sat back for a moment in silence. Then he said, "Make no mistake about it, the results of the Army study were distressing.

34

And the most distressing thing we found is that the men needn't have yielded. Just as they needn't have died in such great numbers. But why don't I let the specialists who took part in the study tell you about those things? Then, when you've finished talking to them, perhaps you'd like to come back, and I can tell you something about what the study taught us in terms of the future."

III

The Voyage Home

General Arthur G. Trudeau—Outline of the Army Study—
Mechanics of Repatriation Process

Major General Arthur G. Trudeau, now a lieutenant general and the Army's Chief of Research and Development, was the next man I called on, the first of a number of uniformed personnel whom I interviewed in the ensuing months about the actual mechanics of the Army study. General Trudeau, a trim, florid, energetic officer, was the Assistant Chief of Staff in charge of G-2, the major division of the service which is charged with the responsibility for intelligence, counterintelligence, and general internal security. (The other large Army sections at the General Staff level are G-1 and G-3 which handle, respectively, the service's personnel and administration and the service's operations and training program.) As the head of what amounts to the Army's detective bureau, General Trudeau was naturally very much concerned with the repatriation of Army

36

prisoners of war who had been exposed to Communist doctrine.

The Army study, Trudeau said, following through on what Milton had already told me about the early propaganda radio talks, was begun soon after the outbreak of hostilities in Korea, with the collecting of tape recordings of all broadcasts by prisoners that were picked up by our monitor stations. Articles written by prisoners that appeared in the Communist press were also clipped and collected. To these exhibits were added data by South Korean intelligence agents employed by us to observe behind the enemy lines; these agents noted and reported pro-Communist acts among American prisoners. Further information about collaboration in prison camps was obtained from those prisoners the Communists released prematurely for propaganda purposes. Some of these men were returned to our lines only a few months after the start of the war, laden with printed leaflets urging our troops to desert. "From the evidence procured in this way, it was obvious that a number of Americans were collaborating," Trudeau said. "We knew what this meant. It meant that upon repatriation of the prisoners there would have to be a complete and unbiased investigation into the whole period of imprisonment of every man. What else could we do? Here was an attempt to subvert thousands of our men to accomplish Communist aims, and on the surface at least there were some indications that it was succeeding. Obviously, we had no other choice than to order a thorough investigation of everyone involved. The

37

security of the country and the security of the service demanded it. And, of course, we knew from the very start that the investigation was going to be a tremendous job."

An important part of the study, Trudeau told me, was naturally devoted to examining the returned prisoners. The Army realized very early in its task that the first step in preparing eventual measures to counteract the treatment our men had received as prisoners would be to obtain from these men as much information as possible about their experiences after capture. When it became clear that repatriation would eventually be accomplished, it was decided to subject each returned man to a series of extensive questions. These would cover not so much military matters—repatriated prisoners are requested, as a matter of routine, to describe any novel types of enemy equipment or installations they may have seen—as, more importantly, the new Communist techniques of handling prisoners. When the men had all been questioned, the resulting data were to be subjected to study by Army experts in various fields.

Within six months after the armistice became a reality in Korea, Trudeau said, a total of 4,435 American prisoners had been released, or had otherwise made their way back, from Communist captivity. There were three groups of prisoners, of which the last and largest arrived after the armistice had actually been signed.

The first group was a heterogeneous batch of 650 who had evaded the Communists, had escaped after having been briefly in their hands, had been liberated from them by combat advances, or had been returned by them for propaganda purposes. The second group consisted of the 149 individuals in *Operation Little Switch*, a mutually agreed upon transfer of sick and wounded made in April, 1953. The third group was made up of the men returned in *Operation Big Switch*, the mass repatriation carried out under the terms of the armistice mostly during August and September, 1953. The men in the first group, except for the few the Communists had sent back for propaganda reasons, had little information to give, since they had been returned before they had ever reached permanent prison camps and in many cases had been absent from their own lines for as little as one or two days. Therefore, interest centered on the men returned in the two Switches. The total of all returned prisoners showed that by services there were 31 Navy, 196 Marine, 235 Air Force, and 3,973 Army personnel; of these last, 3,323 were returned in *Big Switch*. The Army figure, as Trudeau pointed out, was over 89 per cent of the entire prisoner total, which was only to be expected from the nature of the combat operations in Korea.

As progress at the truce talks made it clear that sooner or later our prisoners would be exchanged, the Defense Department designated the Army as the agency to handle the return of these men from the Far East to this country, Trudeau told me. Six months before the actual date of the release of the men in *Big Switch*, the Army had made comprehensive plans for their reception. They were to be collected at a repatriation center, cleaned up and issued new clothes, examined by doctors and intelligence experts, and notified as to details of back pay, leave, and reassignment.

Two things were new in this procedure. For the first time, repatriated prisoners of war were to be given a general psychiatric examination, conducted by medical members of the various services; and for the first time, the emphasis in the intelligence questioning was to be on counterintelligence rather than on military information. Nine Army transports were assigned to bring the men back from Korea to the West Coast.

While these administrative details were being worked out, G-2 began formulating its questionnaire. Seventy multipart counterintelligence questions, covering forty pages, were designed. The purpose of these questions was to determine whether or not a man had succumbed to Communist indoctrination; if he had, how deeply; and by what means and techniques the indoctrination had been accomplished. The questions were carefully phrased, Trudeau said; no man was asked pointblank if he had collaborated. Instead, he was asked for many particulars about his imprisonment—details that, when put together by experienced interrogators and analysts, would give a straightforward and unemotional account of that man's experience as a Communist prisoner, and would reveal whether the man had yielded entirely to indoctrination or only partially, had merely associated with collaborators, or had been completely anti-Communist. Forty-four multipart questions dealing with military information were also devised; these took another thirty-seven pages, and were concerned with such matters as, for example, what the prisoner might have seen of enemy trucks, tanks, and guns, and their workings; of bridges, airfields, and bunkers; and of the respective military roles played by North Koreans, Chinese, and Russians, in North Korea. In addition, an outline was drawn up to record a brief biographical summary of the returned prisoner. The biography was called Phase I; the counterintelligence questions, Phase II; and military intelligence, Phase III.

The Army set up ten groups, called Joint Intelligence Processing Teams, each consisting of seventy-two specialists, to manage the actual return of the prisoners. One team was to sail on each of the nine Army transports; the tenth team was to be based in Japan, to take care of those prisoners who lived in Guam, Hawaii, the Philippines, and other areas west of the United States mainland, or who had to be evacuated by air from Korea to Japan for temporary hospitalization or treatment. The teams included representatives from each of the services, although Army personnel predominated. Each was headed by a board of seven men, composed of four intelligence representatives—one from the Army's counterintelligence division, one from its military intelligence division, one from the Office of Naval Intelligence, and one from the Air Force's Office of Special Investigation, which corresponds to Army counterintelligence—plus one lawyer, usually from the Army's Judge Advocate General's staff, one psychiatrist, and a board

41

chairman from one of the three services. The other members of the team were sixteen military intelligence and sixteen counterintelligence officers, most of them from the Army, who did the interrogating; ten physicians, psychiatrists, and medical helpers; and enough administrative workers to handle the paperwork of restoring the returned prisoners to active status in the ranks of their respective services.

I asked General Trudeau to give me a step-by-step account of how the Army's plan had been put into effect once prisoners began to be returned to us through *Operation Big Switch*. Returnees began to arrive at the repatriation center at Panmunjom about a week after the signing of the armistice, he said, and were moved from there to the embarkation port of Inchon by truck or helicopter, depending on their physical condition. Those who were obviously ill were flown immediately to Japan for medical treatment. Processing of the others began at Inchon, where they were cleaned up and deloused, issued new uniforms, and given a thorough medical checkup; at Inchon additional cases of what appeared to be serious illness were identified and sent to Japan. The medical examination, which took about a half-hour per man, included a chest X-ray, an electrocardiograph, and a blood-pressure test, as well as height and weight measurements, which, of course, the Army could compare with the results of a man's last physical checkup before capture. At Inchon, the returnees were housed in barracks on what had been a Japanese Army post, and were not allowed to mingle with other members of the armed forces.

This was necessary, the Army felt, both from the standpoint of security and for the men's own good, since psychiatrists had advised that the returnees be allowed to become acclimated to freedom gradually.

The Communists released our prisoners in dribs and drabs over a period of more than a month. When there were enough repatriates at Inchon to make a shipload, one of the transports sailed for San Francisco with the men, whose processing was continued on board. During the three-week journey across the Pacific, the intelligence questionnaire was administered to the men. The Army tried to make these questioning sessions more like friendly interviews than interrogations. This was considered very important, Trudeau explained to me. From the prisoners returned earlier by the Communists for propaganda purposes, and from the 149 sick men exchanged in *Operation Little Switch*, the Army had learned that the Communists were warning our men that they would be subjected to intensive and, it was implied, brutal questioning on their return. If our interrogations were not tactfully handled, they would tend to bear out the Communists' warnings, not only about that particular operation, but other, more general warnings about democratic ideas and methods. If the Army had acted hastily or thoughtlessly at this stage, Trudeau pointed out, wavering Americans could easily have been turned into anti-Americans. "Hence our interrogators were asked to be as understanding and sympathetic as possible," he said. "And that is what I think they were."

Before they asked any question, the interrogators explained to the returned prisoner his legal rights. Each man was told that no attempt would be made to get him to give derogatory information about himself, and that such information would not be taken down unless he himself gave it deliberately. Article 31 of the Uniform Code of Military Justice, which states that an individual is not required to make any statement that will tend to incriminate or degrade him, and that he may, if he so chooses, make no statement at all, was repeated to all repatriates. It was, of course, stated at the same time that anything the man did say might be used against him. This blend of openness and consideration on the part of the interrogators would, the Army hoped, convince the former prisoners at the very start that a comfortable way was being prepared by means of which they could return to the standards of loyalty they had once held. After these preliminaries, the interrogators put to the men Phases I, II, and III of the intelligence questionnaire.

Assigned to each shipload of returnees was a psychiatric task force consisting of five psychiatrists, one clinical psychologist, and four enlisted technicians, the last either social workers or psychology experts. Their job was to learn all they could about the psychological conditions under which the prisoners had been held, and the effect these conditions had had upon them. One technique used to find out these things was the psychiatric interview. Each psychiatrist on the team worked from eight in the morning to five in the evening, both at Inchon and on shipboard, holding one-hour consultations with every returned prisoner. Usually the talk was held privately, in a room in the barracks, or in a garden at Inchon, or in a cabin on the ship, and its atmosphere was informal. The doctors customarily made a short speech to begin with, Trudeau told me, that went something like this: "I am Dr. So-and-So. I'm a psychiatrist. My talking to you is only a routine part of the medical examination every returned prisoner is getting. We realize that imprisonment is a difficult thing and that it can cause certain problems. So, first off, we wonder if you have any problems we might help you with. Secondly, we're interested in getting a broad view of prisoners' problems in general, so that we can be of the most possible help to your buddies who will be repatriated after you. Perhaps the best way to start is for you to tell me a little bit about yourself, your home, and what you used to do."

After the man had described his background and life as a civilian, the psychiatrist turned the interview toward his service career, asking such questions as how long had he been in Korea before he was captured, had he been with a good outfit, what took place when he was captured, how did he feel about that, what had he thought was going to happen to him in enemy hands? Usually a pretty good and compact chronological account was obtained in this way, and the psychiatrist could then bring the talk around to what actually had happened to the man in the prison camp. This, of course, was the heart of the interview.

When, in describing his experiences before imprisonment or during it, a man mentioned a detail that was of psychological interest, the psychiatrist would ask him to elaborate on it. For example, a man might remark that he had felt pretty blue on the march to the prison camp. The doctor would then try to get to the bottom of why he felt that way. It might develop that he blamed himself for having been taken prisoner, or that he felt guilty for not having acted as well as he might have toward one of his buddies, who subsequently died. The doctors attached great importance, in forming a psychiatric opinion of the man they were interviewing, to the feelings he described himself as having toward his fellow-prisoners and his captors, to the attitude he expressed toward the interview itself, and to the plans he mentioned for the future. A man who said, for instance, that he planned to take up life right where he had dropped it when he was captured was generally tagged as an immature, unrealistic person, for ordinary life is never the same after a term in prison camp. "One of our psychiatrists used to illustrate that with an anecdote," Trudeau said. "His orderly had been a B-26 gunner in World War II who was shot down over Germany and imprisoned for a couple of years. After the Allied victory, he was released from the prison camp, and his one thought was to get to Paris. But to his great chagrin there was no transportation there for over a month. That man has since told the psychiatrist that the greatest thing that happened to him in the war was having to sit in Germany for a month, slowly getting adjusted to life as a free man. Almost every lesson of that life has to be relearned by a former prisoner."

Not all of the time on the way home was spent in trying

to evaluate a man's prison experiences. The Army realized that the voyage was the right time to offer some elementary mental preparation to help the prisoner face in advance some of the problems that inevitably lay before him. Therefore, aboard ship, group psychotherapy was given to the men in units of fifteen. No attempt was made to dredge up the past; instead, the present situation of a return to a long-awaited promised land was dealt with as realistically as possible. The men were told that, while they were bound for freedom and loved ones, home life in many cases was not going to be like their rosy-colored memories of it. Things would have changed, and they would have changed. They could expect to be heroes momentarily, but only momentarily; and they would have to make plans for a future in which they might be very unheroic—a future in which, incredible as it might seem to them now, the prison camp, where all decisions were made for them, would occasionally appear preferable to the spot in which they might find themselves at home. The object of the therapy was to get them to think and talk realistically about their new existence and in doing so perhaps rid themselves of some of their anxieties about the past and their misconceptions of the future. The psychiatrists found that the group psychotherapy technique as applied to returnees had to differ from the technique used with groups of civilians. With civilian patients, the best results are obtained from passive direction under which the patients themselves bring up and discuss their problems. With the repatriates, who had a tendency to act subdued and dazed in a group, passive direc-

47

tion did not work. Unless the doctor carefully stimulated and actively encouraged general conversation, the men often would not talk at all.

In the psychiatric interview, the doctors were able to make a psychiatric judgment of a man from the way in which he responded to their questions as well as from the answers he gave. Some men were fluent and completely at ease, and said that prison life was hard but bearable. Others found their feelings hard to describe. And some were in a state of hallucination, out of all contact with reality, as, for example, the returned prisoner who gave as his reason for not trying to escape: "Well, there was trouble if you left camp, because you had to find a Chinese soldier to bring you back. They wouldn't let you back inside the lines unless a Chinese soldier brought you. And sometimes you couldn't find a Chinese soldier." The psychiatrist's evaluation of each man's psychological state was summarized in a brief report—usually no more than a few hundred words—which was inserted in the file that was started for each repatriate.

The psychiatrists on each transport had been warned in advance, Trudeau told me, that it looked as if many of the prisoners had been indoctrinated. These indoctrinated men formed the group that the Army and the prisoners themselves called "progressives." Those who resisted the enemy were known as "reactionaries." The Army had emphasized that what it wanted from the psychiatrists was not a judgment on the guilt or innocence of the men they talked to, but information about the state of mind that might have determined these men's actions. The psychiatrists were asked to display neither excessive concern nor hostility, but to try to develop a relationship with each man such as might exist in civilian life between any doctor and patient. Each returned prisoner was also given certain psychological tests to shed further light on his emotional state. The Rorschach test, in which the subject interprets designs formed by ink blots, and the sentence-completion test, in which he rounds out partially formed sentences, were administered by the clinical psychologists and their technician-assistants.

The interviews and tests given the returnees disclosed a low incidence of psychiatric disorders among them. Only a small fraction of those who came back required hospitalization for these causes. The fraction was that—or slightly less than that—which might be expected among the civilian population of any average large American city. This is not to say, however, that the men did not show the effects of their imprisonment. They did, and markedly. Psychologically, the reason seems to be that the majority had yielded in some degree to Communist pressure. No matter how they rationalized this, they knew it was wrong; they knew it betrayed their better nature, and violated the ideals by which they had been reared. Consequently, consciously or unconsciously, they were burdened with guilt, perhaps the most corrosive emotion the human spirit has to bear. Externally their guilt seemed to act on them like a depressant.

For one thing, the returnees displayed much less than

average interest in their environment. Their outlook was a noticeably restricted one, and they expressed few, if any, demands, desires, or wishes for the present, or plans and thoughts about the future. They discussed their lives in an exceedingly flat and unemotional way, using stock phrases over and over again. They were compliant in a negative fashion, and their physical movements and reactions were noticeably slow. Their apathy was not like a psychotic's apathy, which is often abject and massive. These men were capable of response, but their reaction time was measureably delayed, and they showed a limited capacity for elaborating the ideas they expressed.

On the other hand, they were far from lacking in emotion. Beneath this apathetic surface, they were tremendously turbulent, ready to be extremely aggressive, to tear into something and to be angry. The Rorschach tests clearly showed this latent aggressiveness. For instance, repatriates frequently described a certain ink blot as representing two men tearing something apart, sometimes another man's chest from which they were ripping his heart. "Blood," "fire," and "hand grenades" were words that occurred frequently in their psychological sentence-completion tests.

These psychiatric tests and interviews were the first ever given to prisoners of war held by the Communists. They would, the Army feels, form a highly useful standard of comparison should this country ever again be faced with judging prisoners repatriated from a Communist enemy.

IV

Sorting the Data

Repatriates Arrive Home—Process of Sorting Data Started by Army—Methods of Appraisal

The nine shiploads of repatriates arrived at San Francisco between August 15 and September 15, 1953. By the time each ship had completed its three-week voyage across the Pacific, all questionnaires, examinations, interviews, tests, and other details of processing had been finished, and the Joint Intelligence Processing Team in charge of each transport had filed a report with the Army stating its preliminary impressions of the men aboard. At San Francisco, the other services took charge of their men, together with the files that had been assembled on each individual. Army personnel and their files were turned over to the Sixth Army commander, whose headquarters is in San Francisco.

"At this point, the Army study had merely begun," General Trudeau told me. "This was so despite the fact that we had been collecting material for it since 1950 and that the phase that had just closed had required the full-time participation of the seven hundred and twenty members of the Joint Intelligence Processing Teams and the crews of nine Army transports, not to mention numerous other individuals. The onerous job of analyzing the material, which was to occupy scores of experts for over a year, still lay ahead of us. Nobody that I know of has made an accurate calculation of the man-hours consumed by this study, but unquestionably they ran into the millions. No group of men in Army history has ever been so closely studied as these repatriates were."

The Department of the Army ordered the Sixth Army commander to issue thirty-day leaves to all repatriates, and then to reassign them to whatever post was nearest their home. Their files were sent from Sixth Army Headquarters to the various commanders who were ultimately to have jurisdiction over them. Each field commander was to summarize, from the files of each of the men now in his charge, Phase II and III of the intelligence questionnaire, and to send copies of these summaries to all other field commanders. The Phase III summaries on military intelligence concerning North Korea were simply for the other officers' general information. From the Phase II, or counterintelligence summaries, each commander was able to learn what other prisoners had said about any of the men who had just come under his command. The Army felt it wise, Trudeau explained, for field commanders to have as soon as possible some advance data, both good and bad, on repatriates who would be serving under him, and the summarizing method seemed the quickest way of doing it. The files, with the summaries made by each commander, were then sent to the Department of the Army in Washington. Here they were turned over to G-2, in October of 1953, for detailed study and appraisal.

The first task of correlating the data in the Army study was simply one of cross-referencing names. This kept twenty persons in a special section of G-2 busy, often fifteen and eighteen hours a day, for over six months. Each repatriate in the course of his intelligence questionnaire had mentioned the names of men whom he believed to have military intelligence of special value to the government; and more importantly, each man had named many other prisoners as having committed acts, both good and bad, in the prison camps. Some files contained hundreds of names; one had nearly a thousand. Each reference to another prisoner had to be excerpted from the questionnaire of the man who made it, and placed on a separate sheet in the file of the man about whom it was made. Establishing the validity of statements made by prisoners about each other was perhaps the most critical part of the Army study, General Trudeau told me. "Anyone who has had experience in correlating the reports of witnesses, even about something as trivial as a street fight, will understand the delicacy of this," he said. "Opinions differ and errors of judgment occur with even the most scrupulously honest and unbiased observers." It is easy to imagine, then, the difficulties of trying to determine the truth about what happened in a prison camp when the only sources were men, many of them vengeful and guilt-ridden, who had often been divided into cliques, and some of whom were willing to lie about others in order to help themselves.

To evaluate the material in the fairest possible manner, legally trained personnel in G-2 set up standards to guide the workers who were assigned to its special investigating section. "For example," the General said, "they were told to rate highly a man's positive admission that he had signed papers allowing his name to be used in enemy propaganda leaflets calling for peace or surrender, or that he had seen another man actually sign such papers. If he said he had seen another man sign, it was, of course, necessary to assess the accuser's credibility as a witness in the light of what others had said about *him*, as well as to consider the statements of others about the man he was denouncing. Such verification was extremely important. If we had taken as a basis for judgment the statements of two collaborators, for instance, who knew each other and who talked about each other, without consulting any other sources, those men would have emerged as two of the greatest heroes of the Korean War."

The search for verification frequently led an investigator a merry chase. If a man, either in denouncing or commending another man, said his statement could be supported by a certain red-haired lieutenant who had been in such-and-such platoon of a prison camp, the investigator would have

to try to locate the file of the red-haired lieutenant by following clues in other prisoners' files, or by checking Army
personnel records for a man corresponding to his physical
description. Once located, the red-haired lieutenant's file
was checked for confirmation of the first man's statement.
If none was found there, the lieutenant himself had to be
interviewed directly, and asked by the investigator to af-
firm or deny the statement. Many anonymous red-haired
lieutenants cropped up in G-2's research. "The investigators," Trudeau continued, "were told to give a low rating
to such unsupported and arbitrary statements as that a certain man was an informer or that a certain man preferred
Communism to democracy. And the number of positive
statements, both derogatory and complimentary, a man
made were also an important factor in ascertaining his
loyalty."

I asked General Trudeau about some of the other criteria
by which the Army judged a man's loyalty, or the degree to
which he had collaborated.

"I'll give you two examples," he said. "One was the information the returnee supplied about what offices he had
held in camp, and what his duties and privileges had been.
Broadly speaking, the more he yielded to the Communists,
the higher were the positions he was given—although his
lot as a prisoner, in matters like food and shelter, was not
necessarily improved by this collaboration. For another
thing, by the time prisoners were returned in *Operation Big
Switch*, the Army had been given the names of many men

accused of collaboration, cooperation, and informing by early returnees and *Little Switch* men who had been processed after they reached home. Our interrogators made use of these names in questioning the *Big Switch* returnees, and their reaction to the names was another criterion. For instance, when a prisoner who had been at a heavily indoctrinated camp for a long time was asked if he had seen evidences of collaboration, cooperation, or informing, and on the part of whom, he might name only one or two of the men who we knew very well had been friendly to the enemy. In that case, the interrogator would question him again more thoroughly, going over the same ground carefully. If he still suppressed the names of major collaborators, there was a good chance that the man himself was one, and this was noted by the interrogator in the report he made at the end of each questionnaire. Evidence of this kind was, of course, taken very seriously by the G-2 investigators evaluating the case."

There were 215 cases among men still in the Army, as compared with 210 cases among those discharged, in which preliminary screening indicated further study was necessary to determine whether serious acts of collaboration or other misconduct requiring court-martial had been committed. The charges which, if substantiated, would merit such action included informing on fellow-prisoners; mistreatment or causing the mistreatment of fellow-prisoners; aiding the enemy's propaganda program by writing or signing peace petitions, making broadcasts or circulating peace petitions for other prisoners to sign; cooperating in the Communist indoctrination program; and attempting to get other prisoners to accept and follow Communism.

Beginning in the spring of 1954, more than six months were devoted to study and further research on these 215 cases by a specially selected group of legal, intelligence, and combat officers. "All the standards applied in the preliminary study were maintained and more rigorously applied by this group," Trudeau told me. "In addition, further evidence was procured to aid these officers in making their judgments. From the government stations that intercept and record foreign radio broadcasts, they got transcripts of every message sent out over every Communist station in eastern Asia, in the actual words of the speaker, during the period of the Korean War. From intelligence teams that had been concerned with analyzing Communist propaganda efforts in the Far East, they obtained copies of all the Communist documents distributed among United States forces in the combat line, some of which had been written by the men whose cases were under review, or had been signed by them. Besides this, they got hold of every issue of the Shanghai *Daily News*, and of many other Communist periodicals that had been published in Asia during the period from the start of the war to the end of it, and combed these for articles by or about American prisoners. Copies of any information on the men collected by other governmental agencies, such as the F.B.I., were acquired. More important than all this further evidence, however, was the fact that the

57

cases were being reassessed in the light of the experience
of these mature and specially trained officers. The two
hundred and fifteen cases were those of men who seemed
to have erred. Just how plausible did the excuses they offered
for their conduct seem to these seasoned officers? And how
did these excuses hold up in the light of the men's own
actions? For instance, if a man said he had acted as he did
for the good of another prisoner, was it actually the other
prisoner who was benefited or was it the man himself? Did
the statements of witnesses support or refute the man's
own statements, and were these witnesses reliable and in a
position to have the knowledge they claimed to have?
Evaluation—though admittedly very, very complex—was
possible."

General Trudeau cited one example to show how carefully statements had to be checked. In the psychiatric interview given on the boat coming home, a certain sergeant
had told Lieutenant Colonel Paul M. Schrader, of the Army
Medical Corps, that he regarded the Chinese Communists
as dishonest, not ever to be trusted, and that he thought
they were savages. When his record was thoroughly gone
into, it was found that 185 fellow-prisoners had mentioned
this sergeant as a collaborator, and that in propaganda
broadcasts to the United States, recorded by our stations,
he had declared that he could never say enough for the
Chinese Volunteer Forces in Korea, whose kind, consider-
ate, humane treatment had saved his life, and who had
given him food, comfort, and peace as a prisoner, and oper-

ated their prisoner compounds along the restful lines of a summer camp. Among the 185 prisoners who made derogatory statements about this man were men who reported that he had announced publicly he would sacrifice his American citizenship, if necessary, to fight for Communism, and others who said that his improper distribution of food had contributed to the death of some men from malnutrition. Approximately eighty-five additional statements, also derogatory, were deemed too lacking in support to be put into the sergeant's record, largely because the men who made them had misspelled or shortened his last name. Incidentally, Trudeau told me, the figure of 185 statements was about average for the number of derogatory statements made about any of the 215 men whose cases were being considered by these officers. One man had over 800 such statements made about him.

To make sure that every last bit of relevant information that could be obtained was available to the officers before they passed on their recommendations, the Army ordered a Report of Investigation on each of the 215 cases under consideration. Army intelligence agents interviewed every man, whether still in the service or out of it, who had made a derogatory statement about any of the 215. If the man was able to expand or document his original charge, the information was taken down in the form of a sworn statement. The Reports of Investigation in some cases contained as many as 300 sworn statements, from men all over the United States. To cut down travel time and expense in collecting these reports, the Army classified potential interviewees according to the Army command in which they were located, and agents from that command interviewed them and forwarded the results to Washington.

During the course of its lengthy investigation, the Army was naturally confronted time and again with problems both foreseen and unforeseen, some large and some small. One small, unforeseen problem, General Trudeau said, arose shortly after the repatriates had landed at San Francisco. It was decided that it would be a good idea, for general intelligence purposes, to have the military and counter-intelligence phases of the files of the almost 3,400 *Big Switch* Army returnees duplicated and sent to all the major United States and global commanders and to certain other departments. It was decided to make twenty copies of each of the two phases, and bids on the more than two million pages were obtained for copying by all methods, including mimeographing, master dittoing, stencilling, lithographing, offset printing, and photostating. Depending on the method, the cost ranged from close to a million dollars to fifty thousand. The Army was dismayed. Even the lowest figure was prohibitive, and the plan for copying and distributing that portion of the files was dropped.

I asked General Trudeau if I could see what a returned prisoner's file looked like, and he had one brought in and placed on his desk. The file was a formidable stack of paper, about as thick as an unabridged dictionary, topped with a blue paper cover. The sheets were of various colors and sizes,

the largest approximately legal size. The whole was bound
firmly together at the top with an adjustable metal fastener.
"This is not an especially thick file," General Trudeau said.
"Some are close to two feet thick, but some of those on
prisoners who were taken very late in the war or against
whom there was no derogatory information are less than an
inch thick." I asked the General to list the contents for me.
In this one, he said, leafing though it, there were the eighty-
odd pages of the three-phase intelligence questionnaire, plus
summaries of Phases II and III. In some cases, he told me,
in which the answers to the Phase III intelligence questions had suggested that the returnee possessed extraordi-
nary information, a Phase IV, a long-range strategic-intelli-
gence questionnaire had been administered, covering data
such as details of enemy airfield construction. Next in this
file came the psychiatric evaluation. Then there were copies
of statements by other prisoners about this man, and, since
in this case these statements were mostly derogatory, a Report of Investigation by Army intelligence agents. There
were copies of enemy propaganda leaflets and peace and
surrender petitions that this man had signed, and transcripts
of broadcasts made by him over the Communist radio;
copies of information on this man collected by government
agencies other than the Army; and sworn statements made
by the individual himself. The record of the repatriate's
medical examination, the General said, was in the Surgeon
General's office.

When the files are not in official use, they are kept in the

Army's Central Records Facility, at Fort Holabird, in Baltimore, Maryland. This one-story concrete building, which has 49,000 square feet of floor area, is the main repository for all intelligence data on military and civilian service personnel. The repatriates' files are stored there in 210 foot lockers, from fifty to two hundred to a box, depending on their size. The files are taken from Fort Holabird to Washington and the nearby Second Army Headquarters and back by motor vehicle, under the care of an armed courier; registered mail is used for forwarding them to more distant Army headquarters.

V

The Treason Trials

Records of Some Repatriates Studied for Possible Court-martial Action—The Court-martial Summary—No Department of Justice Action to be Taken Against Dischargees

"The national security was very much on our minds here at G-2 as the Army study developed," General Trudeau told me. "We were in an extremely difficult position in some ways. But in a position that we have felt we have had to maintain and expand, for, as it seems to us here, the good of us all. We wanted to do justice both to the country and to the returnees themselves. In order to do this, certain decisions had to be taken."

After the cross-referencing and the preliminary evaluations had been completed by G-2 early in 1954, the 3,323 files of the Army repatriates were divided into two groups: those men who were still in the service, and those who had been discharged. The two groups were practically equal in number, with 1,644 men still in service and 1,679 dischargees. A summary of the file on each of the men who had been discharged was sent to the office of the Federal Bureau of Investigation in the area in which the man lived, for the simple reason that all prisoners had been exposed to Communist propaganda. Two hundred and ten of the dischargees' summaries contained material that, in the opinion of the Army, might give the F.B.I. reason to investigate those particular men more thoroughly as possible security risks, or might cause the Department of Justice to examine the cases for possible criminal action against the men as civilians. "Our study of the files of the relatively small group of suspect returnees who were still in service continued. In a handful of the cases it ended in court-martial," Trudeau told me. "Meanwhile, our policy was to follow the uncourt-martialed suspects over whom we had jurisdiction through their various assignments, hoping, until it was proved otherwise, that their loyalty had not been affected by the Communist indoctrination. The last thing in the world we wanted was to prejudice, without due cause, the service careers or the future lives of any returnees. As far as those still in the Army are concerned, we expect to see to it that they are not treated, as a group, in any special or disparaging manner."

For more than six months the officers assigned to the second G-2 study group examined the files of the 1,644 prisoners remaining in the service. Two hundred and fifteen cases (as compared to the 210 referred to the F.B.I.) were selected as deserving further study before a decision was made as to whether general court-martial was warranted. Eventually 82 of these cases were approved for court-martial, and the rest were dismissed for lack of enough supporting evidence to be considered for such serious action.

The 82 approved cases were then brought before the Army's Board on Prisoners of War Collaboration. This board had been set up early in 1954 by joint action of the Chief of Staff and the Secretary of the Army, as the first in a four-unit chain of review whose functions were to safeguard the legal rights of those under investigation, and to see that only appropriate cases were brought to trial. If a case was approved for trial by this board, it was then reviewed by the Assistant Chief of Staff, G-1, the Army section charged with discipline and questions of morale; if it was passed by this officer, the case went to Mr. Milton as the appropriate Assistant Secretary of the Army, and from him to the Assistant Secretary of Defense in charge of manpower, the official who had the responsibility of finally approving the case for trial. From this, General Trudeau remarked, I could see that cases were not brought to trial by any hasty or ill-considered procedure.

The cases of 47 men out of the 82 that were scrutinized were finally approved for general court-martial by the four-level Pentagon reviewing authority. Twelve of the men were actually brought to trial before tribunals sitting at various Army command posts around the country. In addition, two other repatriates were tried by court-martial before the Army initiated the four-level reviewing procedure early in 1954. The crimes of which the accused men were charged included informing on fellow prisoners, collaborating with the Communist enemy, misconduct as a prisoner of war, assault on an officer, larceny, and murder.

The prisoners were tried, I was told, because the Army took the position that its men are responsible for their actions as prisoners of war just as they are responsible for their actions in all other military and civilian situations. The court proceedings against the prisoners precipitated a spate of plays—radio, television, and theatrical—as well as much book and magazine fiction. Most of these literary efforts presented sympathetically the unquestioned misfortunes that the captives had undergone, and the way they were received showed that large segments of the public were by no means convinced that the Army's position was correct.

The justification for the trials was outlined for me by Lieutenant Colonel Charles M. Trammell, Jr., a plans and policy officer who was serving as special counsel to the G-2 section. "The trials were, after all, a matter of simple logic," he said. "The Army had formulated certain policies for the conduct of its personnel which it believed to be the right ones. These included a prisoner's giving no aid or comfort to the enemy, and his abiding by the rules of the Code of Military Justice. The important question during the trials, as far as the Army was concerned, was not whether the Army should continue to use such disciplinary machinery. Disciplinary machinery in itself is merely one of the powers of government which are used to enforce necessary law and order, without which society can't endure. The knotty and fundamental problem, of course, was the original working out of the policies of conduct and the minimum standards that these policies called for. Once these had been agreed upon, the decision had to be supported consistently thereafter by all the disciplinary machinery at the Army's command—or these policies, and other Army policies, would become completely meaningless."

The results of the courts-martial, which took place before a panel of officers belonging to the same command as the accused, were eleven convictions and three acquittals. The sentences imposed by the tribunals ranged from life imprisonment to a mere reprimand with freezing in rank for two years. Under the mandatory review that takes place by the commanding officer of all courts-martial decreeing punishment, one sentence of life imprisonment was reduced to twenty years, one sentence of eight years was reduced to two-and-a-half years, and one sentence of fifteen years was reduced to one year. Life imprisonment was recommended continued in a conviction for murder, and other punishments were ordered approved.

After the mandatory review by the commanding officer, another examination of all punishments was made in the Pentagon by the Board of Review of the Judge Advocate General's Department of the Army, an action which also is mandatory. The Board of Review reduced one previously approved sentence of forty years to ten years, one of five years to two-and-a-half years, and affirmed sentence in the other cases. Petition for a final review of penalty, which any convicted court-martial defendant has the right to make, was made in eight cases, which went to the Court of Military Appeals. This body, whose position in the Army corresponds to that of the United States Supreme Court in civilian affairs, handed down decisions in the eight cases that had the effect of confirming previous judgment.

The Army's prisoner-of-war trials have now been completed.

The trials were generally unpopular; in addition, a decided sentiment existed among the public that the Army was throwing the book at the enlisted men and letting the officers off scot-free, or virtually so. Nine enlisted men were tried, and eight convicted; five officers were tried, and three convicted. The original sentences handed down by the courts-martial to the enlisted men ranged from terms of two years to life imprisonment. Of the three guilty officers, one was sentenced to dismissal from the service, forfeiture of all pay and allowances, and given confinement at hard labor for ten years; one was dismissed with forfeiture of pay and allowances; and one was reprimanded and frozen in rank for two years. These facts did seem to lend weight to the public's feelings.

I asked Trammell whether he could explain this. He said that, unfortunately, he did not have any pat answer, and that he had not been at the trials. He did, however, offer the following background information which, he said, might conceivably explain the courts' actions. "Three types of cases came before them," Trammell told me. "The first involved general collaboration with the enemy; the second, criminal acts against fellow prisoners; and the third, misleading fellow prisoners or failing to lead them when duty required proper leadership. Officers were tried on charges arising out of both categories one and three. But we have no record of any officer committing a provable criminal act against a fellow prisoner in Korea. This, of course, is a particularly distasteful offense to Americans. It is emotionally highly charged for those who sit in judgment on the case, and, often, can be more easily proved than violations of the two other types. This charge of criminal acts against fellow prisoners was a common accusation among the enlisted cases tried. Moreover, in the case of the officers all, except one, pleaded in self-defense that they had acted under the direction of a superior officer. These factors, in conjunction with the lack of a charge of criminal acts against fellow prisoners in the case of the officers tried, may well have had some effect on the courts' decisions, and produced the impression among the public that the trials were weighted against the enlisted man."

Trammell suggested that if I looked at the transcripts of some of the trials, this point might be clearer. I did so, and found, for example, that the following were the three most serious of the ten charges against James C. Gallagher, an enlisted man, whose life sentence for murder was the most severe of any meted out to a former prisoner after the Army had instituted its four-level reviewing practice:

Specification 1: In that Sergeant (then Corporal) James C. Gallagher, US Army, Headquarters and Headquarters Detachment, 1201st Area Service Unit, did, at Prisoner of War Camp No. 5, in the vicinity of Pyoktong, North Korea, on or about February 1951 murder Corporal Donald Thomas Baxter, an American prisoner of war, by means of forcibly ejecting him from his place of shelter and causing him to be exposed to extremely cold temperature, the said Corporal Donald Thomas Baxter at that time being sick, infirm with dysentery, and unable to help himself.

Specification 2: In that Sergeant (then Corporal) James C. Gallagher, US Army, Headquarters and Headquarters Detachment, 1201st Area Service Unit, did, at Prisoner of War Camp No. 5, in the vicinity of Pyoktong, North Korea, on or about February 1951 murder Corporal John William Jones, an American prisoner of war, by means of forcibly ejecting him from his place of shelter and causing him to be exposed to extremely cold temperature, the said Corporal John William Jones at that time being sick, infirm with dysentery, and unable to help himself.

Specification 3: In that Sergeant (then Corporal) James C. Gallagher, US Army, Headquarters and Headquarters Detachment, 1201st Area Service Unit, did, at Prisoner of War Camp No. 5, in the vicinity of Pyoktong, North Korea, on or about March 1951 murder an American prisoner of war, name unknown, by means of striking him about the body; by forcibly suspending him from a hook on the wall, leaving him to so hang with his feet off the ground, and thereafter forcibly ejecting him from his place of shelter and causing him to be exposed to extremely cold temperature, the said unidentified American prisoner of war at that time being sick, infirm from dysentery, and unable to help himself.

When I looked into the courtroom records of the two senior officers tried, both lieutenant colonels, I found considerably milder forms of wrongdoing alleged. One was accused of revealing to the Communists the conversation of four prisoners, thus causing the four to be sent, to their detriment, to a punishment camp; but he was convicted only of taking part in indoctrination classes for prisoners and of making propaganda helpful to the enemy. He was dismissed from the service with forfeiture of all pay and allowances.

The second man, the senior officer among those tried, was charged with making disloyal statements to prisoners, leading Communist discussion groups, and writing and broadcasting propaganda statements. He was convicted, however, merely of making enemy propaganda, and ordered reprimanded and frozen in rank for two years.

The text of this officer's reprimand is as follows:

You, Lieutenant Colonel —— — ——, having been found guilty by a general court-martial of the offenses of aiding and of knowingly communicating, corresponding, and holding intercourse with the enemy, while a prisoner of war during the Korean conflict, by making recordings that were inimicable to the interests of the United States, and having, by said court-martial, been sentenced, among other things, to a reprimand, are hereby reprimanded.

The court-martial, by its sentence, could have sentenced you to dismissal, imprisonment, and forfeiture of all pay and allowances. It is your good fortune that the court-martial limited its punishment to suspension from rank for twenty-four months and to a reprimand. Your conduct, as reflected in the findings of the court-martial, and as fully supported by the record of your trial, discloses that you, an officer of the Regular Army, with the advantage of an education tendered you by the people of the United States in the United States Military Academy at West Point, with a background of many years of service in various ranks and assignments in the United States Army, and in spite of the full and positive knowledge that you must have gained by your education and experience, as above outlined, of the conduct expected and required of an officer, supinely complied with the dictates of your captors and otherwise conducted yourself in a servile, craven, and unsoldierly manner for the obvious purpose of securing favored treatment for yourself while a prisoner of war. Although you well knew that your participation in the armed conflict did not end when you were taken prisoner, and that it was your positive duty to carry on the conflict to the best of your ability as a prisoner of war, offering only that degree of cooperation contemplated by international law and holding yourself ever in readiness to escape and resume the fight, you chose to damn your country and its representatives, to hold the American way of life up to ridicule and contempt, and to extoll the practices and concepts of a deadly enemy. In committing this heinous crime you made recordings at the request of said enemy, the purpose of which was fully known to you, namely, to use as a psychological warfare weapon against your country and its forces. The odiousness of your actions and of your philosophy is clearly evidenced when compared with the steadfastness and the fortitude displayed by many other officers and enlisted men, including many of very limited service, in refusing information to, or cooperation of any kind or description with, their unprincipled captors. Furthermore, the conduct of which you stand convicted occurred at a time when other, and loyal, American soldiers and officers were fighting and dying in the defense of the United States. You have held personal safety and comfort above duty, honor, and country, and, in so doing, have

72

deliberately violated your oath as a citizen of the United States and as an officer of the United States Army. Your actions have not only brought disgrace upon yourself, but upon the Army and upon all of those who wear its uniform, and have caused me to harbor the gravest doubts as to your fitness for continued membership and service in the United States Army.

> a/ Robert N. Young
> Lieutenant General, USA
> Commanding
> Headquarters, Sixth Army

Thirty-five of the 47 cases originally approved for court-martial never came to trial, I learned from Trammell. In each instance, the field commander, as was his privilege, went on record as stating that basis for reasonable doubt in applying so stringent a measure existed, although it is hard for a detached observer to see why. To begin with, the 35 untried cases were part of 215 carefully culled from thousands that had been studied for over a year by the two specially constituted G-2 study groups. They were among 82 cases of the more flagrant violations discovered in the 215, which had been presented for judgment to the four-level reviewing authority in the Pentagon. Thirty-five of these cases, as noted earlier, were disallowed. This second batch of 35 that I am now discussing, however, along with the twelve that actually reached trial, were unanimously approved by the four-level reviewing chain, starting with the Army's Board of Prisoner of War Collaboration and ending with the Assistant Secretary of Defense for Manpower, Personnel, and Reserve.

On the other hand, there is no question that the trials were widely unpopular, if, from the Army's point of view, widely misunderstood. The picture the public had during this period—a picture almost impossible to correct—was of a large, brutal Army picking on a small, defenseless former prisoner. This picture had another aspect, also—the thoughts certain segments of the public had about how they themselves might have reacted under prisoner-of-war circumstances. Each trial brought more publicity, most of which was highly unwelcome to the service. Under these circumstances, it is understandable, if not exactly commendable, that the field commanders concerned failed to bring court-martial proceedings—they were, perhaps, doing what the Army has more than once been accused of doing, namely, taking the easy way out.

The remaining 35 cases were disposed of by "boarding" —an Army term for a process less drastic than court-martial whereby an administrative military board decides whether the actions of a respondent require that he should be separated from the service for its good and, if so, whether by an honorable, general, or undesirable discharge, or some other way. Rather surprisingly, it would seem, in the light of the charges, the administrative boards decreed 26 honorable discharges. Eight of the nine men who were left were eliminated through general or undesirable discharges, by accepting the resignation of a commission, or by relief from active duty. One case is still to be decided.

Bell, Cowart, and Griggs, the first of twenty-one turncoats who changed their minds and returned from Red China, were held in custody by the Army when they first entered the country. Subsequently, however, the Army released them following a Supreme Court decision, in a somewhat parallel military case, that apparently made the trio civilians. Their records were then turned over to the Department of Justice for possible action against them as civilians by that branch of the government. For their part, Bell, Cowart, and Griggs promptly instituted legal action against the government for the recovery of back pay allegedly owed them as prisoners. At this writing, the suit is still pending before the United States Court of Claims.

It now appears certain that nothing will be done about Bell, Cowart, and Griggs, nor about the 210 other discharged prisoners of war whom the Army thought might properly be considered for civilian trial by the Department of Justice. After studying the matter for several years the Department of Justice has recently concluded that prosecutions would be impractical. The Department feared it had little chance at this date to bring them to a successful conclusion. One of the important considerations in the decision was the belief that time had necessarily dimmed the memory of prospective witnesses concerning events about which they would be called upon to testify. Therefore, the punishment of collaborators, both in and out of the military service, now seems legally over.

VI

Espionage for the Enemy

Espionage Missions—Seventy-five Repatriates Involved—Army
Men Still Unaccounted For in Communist Hands

The scope and completeness of the Army study uncovered several situations which, although relatively minor
in regard to the number of men involved, properly come
within any inclusive report of that investigation. One of the
more serious of these was that the Army found that certain
of our soldiers had been so thoroughly indoctrinated by the
Communists that they had been recruited to act as spies,
and had returned from prison with definite missions as
enemy agents in the United States.

To answer my questions about this aspect of the study,
the Army put me in touch with Captain Bert Cumby, a
slender intelligence officer in his middle thirties. Cumby,
then stationed at Fort Holabird in Baltimore and now on
duty in West Germany, was in charge of a special interroga-

tion team of three officers in the Army's Far East Command which handled the more important intelligence interviews with returnees during the reprocessing of the former prisoners. "Naturally we wondered ahead of time whether some of our people would come back as spies, for that is standard Communist practice," Cumby told me. "For example, from the talks which our intelligence officers had had with the Japanese who were held captive in Siberia in the Second World War, we learned that both the Chinese and the Russians had recruited a huge number of potential agents from among this group of prisoners and assigned to them tasks to be fulfilled on return to Japan. The fact that they had enrolled so large a number showed that they expected the attrition rate to be very high. As a matter of fact, we have learned that it was estimated by the Communists that the loss would be as great as two-thirds. But they also evidently assumed some degree of success that would make the effort worthwhile. In the Far East intelligence section, during reprocessing, we were naturally very much on the lookout for such espionage agents among American returnees. Actually, some seventy-five did turn up on initial and subsequent screening, either in the Orient or on the high seas before getting back to port in the United States. They were well prepared, we found, for their assignments. They had codes and fairly explicit instructions as to how to reach and recognize their future contacts—equipment that revealed how substantial was the planning that had gone into this project and how protracted the aims the Communists had in mind for these men. For example, they were instructed to make their initial contact, in most cases, only after six or seven years had passed after their return to the United States. The very first man we uncovered in this group followed this predominant pattern. As it happened, he went into great detail after his discovery in telling us about what his duties were to be as a Communist agent. These were to begin after a long initial period of quiet, and were to last five years. After describing the assignments to us minutely, he then handed over the codes that he had. We were quite impressed with the concrete details of his account. This initial discovery showed that, as had been the case with the Japanese, the enemy planning was of a very long-range nature, yet quite specific over this long range. The men comprising the group that was uncovered were for the most part sleepers—that is, persons who had never committed any acts in the prison camps that would mark them as being especially pro-Communist. Because of this protective coloration it would have been extremely difficult for us to ferret them out later had they originally slipped by us. A further difficulty was that the men were instructed to behave in a highly conforming sort of way for a good many years after repatriation, attracting no attention, and certainly not engaging in any radical activities. The enemy had not only re-educated this entire group of captives to come back and spy of their own free will against their country, but this re-education was so successful that it stuck—except in the few cases of those who confessed.

Fortunately for us, their confessions implicated the others. We should, I think, be careful neither to overestimate nor to underestimate this. We knew it was a possibility to begin with; and we were completely prepared for the possibility. Provision has been made, of course, for these men to be carefully watched in the future. Actually, the majority probably do not realize that they are known Communist agents.

"You may wonder," Cumby continued, "how most of the people we know were given espionage missions were not identified as having been progressives in the camps. They were people who were perhaps fence-sitters, or who perhaps even acted in a reasonably reactionary manner. How could these men have been separated from their comrades long enough for them to have been re-educated to the status of a somewhat trained intelligence agent without their campmates being aware that something strange was going on? Actually, it was quite simple. In an appreciable number of the cases uncovered in questioning the returnees during the repatriation process, men would report that they knew so-and-so in their camp until a certain date, and then he just disappeared. They stated they never saw him again, although they heard he was repatriated. He would, of course, turn up in another camp. Getting exact dates and finding out how long these particular men were absent from any particular camp was a practical impossibility during repatriation; but in checking along these lines later in the cases of certain suspects, some important clues turned up that ultimately helped us. The device of a transfer from camp to camp—and, of course, no check was possible to the other prisoners on where their comrades stayed between camps—provides the explanation of how agents received their indoctrination and their training. They were finally returned to new camps, often posing as mild reactionaries, without any of their fellow-prisoners being at all the wiser."

Corporal Claude J. Batchelor, one of the first convicted collaborators among the Army prisoners, was one of the seventy-five men who returned as enemy agents. Batchelor had been one of the original twenty-three prisoners who had early announced that they were going to stay in Communist hands, a figure that was later reduced to twenty-one. Therefore, along with a relatively few others among the seventy-five, he had been an actual progressive, and so was an exception to the rule that progressives were not spies. His assignment was to head a unit in this country to be called "The Ex-Prisoners-of-War Welfare Organization." His testimony on this at his court-martial received little, if any, publicity.

Because he had questioned Batchelor in the Far East, Cumby was a government witness at Batchelor's trial at Fort Sam Houston, Texas. It was the first instituted by the Army against Communist collaborators. When the trial opened, it aroused strong and vocal public opposition. Americans who may have considered themselves, with good reason, to be highly patriotic citizens voiced decided anti-Army opinions about the proceedings. Cumby received two letters while he was at Fort Sam Houston threatening

his life if he took the stand against Batchelor. Because
Cumby is a Negro and Batchelor a white man, such com-
munications might have been regarded as pure instances
of racism in Texas, were it not for the fact that the chief
prosecutor, a white colonel, received an average of twenty-
five hostile letters a day. One of them, Cumby told me,
was the most scurrilous he has ever seen. It came from the
vice-president of an oil company who stated in unprintable
language that he was going to see that the Federal Bureau
of Investigation conducted an inquiry into the motives of
every officer who took part in the trial on the government
side, including the court members. After Batchelor's conviction, the prosecuting colonel left immediately on leave
because both he and the Army felt that local resentment
against him was rising beyond control, and he did not return
to duty at the camp until public opinion about the judgment
had died down. "The trial was a necessary procedure and,
in my opinion, a right procedure," Cumby told me, "but
frankly it was one of the worst experiences I've ever had.
I would not want to go through the like again."

In defense of those who berated the Army for taking a
tough attitude toward delinquent prisoners, it must be said
that there is some basis for their attitude, a basis furnished,
ironically enough, by the Army itself. "The public was not
told at first that there had been disloyal prisoners," said
Cumby. "This is unfortunate but true. When repatriation
began, everybody in America was led to think that the returnees were all heroes. First impressions, regrettably, are

the strongest. Until the true facts are presented as forcibly as were those original half-facts, the impression that the Army was unfair and bullying when it instituted these trials will probably remain in the minds of many Americans."

As the prisoners came out of Communist hands in the Far East during repatriation, Cumby said, the Army clamped a strict censorship on news, primarily to protect the innocent against false charges of collaboration until its own official investigation could get under way. Otherwise, many serious accusations would have been made and publicized. Every hut and every compound, the Army knew, was riddled with cliques and feuds, and there was no way to tell which charges were right and which were wrong without careful research. As a result, the only information released to the press was highly favorable to the repatriates, and minutely detailed the unquestioned hardships they had undergone. Adulatory stories based on this material, glorifying the men and giving the impression that the prisoners as a whole were a courageous and patriotic lot simply because they had weathered their experiences and come back alive, were written and published. The dark part of the picture was completely suppressed, as the case of Corporal Edward S. Dickenson illustrates perfectly. "While he was still behind the Bamboo Curtain as one of the twenty-three GI's who originally refused repatriation," Cumby said, "scores of the newly-freed prisoners wanted to expose him to newspapermen. His camp-mates were full of resentment against him for his treatment of them and they had well-

82

authenticated records of his offenses. But the stories they could have supplied—which would have provided the public at an early date with some indication of what was to come in the way of courts-martial and probable convictions—were prohibited by censorship for the general good of all the prisoners."

A second factor, which also involved Batchelor and Dickenson, further incited opposition to the trials. "To prompt the twenty-three original turncoats to reconsider, the Army directed propaganda broadcasts at them which stated that if they complied with the request to return, no charges of desertion would be placed against them. Under the military code, their previous refusal to report for duty was desertion," Cumby said. "The tape recordings of these broadcasts prove that the Army did not state that it would exonerate these men for other misdeeds committed as prisoners. The offers, however, were misconstrued by many Americans, including at least one Congressman, as being pledges of general amnesty. When Dickenson returned, there was no question but that he should be tried. He was one of our most flagrant collaborators. More than one hundred of his fellow-prisoners accused him of collaboration and informing. Yet when the public information officer in the Pentagon released the announcement of Dickenson's forthcoming court-martial, that officer received so many threats against his life that he asked for and received permission to carry a pistol for his own personal safety. That was right here in Washington. It's a revelation of how uninformed the public attitude was on these matters. Ignorance of the facts accounts for all of the hostility to the trials, I would say. Or to put it another way, poor Army public relations is at the bottom of it—public relations being a field, I guess, in which the Army has a lot to learn."

Another point—also somewhat off the main track of the service's prisoner-of-war study but nevertheless a matter of great importance to all Americans—is that the Army discovered in its investigation that 244 of its men who went into Korea are still unaccounted for (out of a total of 450 from all services). This figure is in addition to the 2,634 Army personnel who were known to have died in captivity and the 1,036 others authenticated as victims of battlefield atrocities. Unfortunately, we do not know how many—if any—of these men are still alive. If any are, Cumby reminded me, they are, of course, illegally retained captives and thus, in essence, kidnap victims.

"We don't find it surprising that some of our men are unaccounted for," Cumby said. "Communist countries have always withheld captives after a war for the benefits they could bring Communism. These benefits, of course, are numerous and obvious. Large numbers of prisoners are used, as were thousands of Germans and Japanese prisoners in Russia in World War II, as slave laborers. Relatively small numbers of prisoners, such as the two hundred and forty-four unaccounted-for Army men, could be used politically. Foreign radio announcers, for instance, are scarce behind the Iron Curtain. Under duress some kidnapees in the past have been known to do such work in Communist countries. To pick another benefit at random, the identities and biographies of our men would be handy for supplying counterfeit personalities and passport data to Communist agents who wish to pose as Americans, something they could do whether our men were alive or dead. Considering the matter in a purely practical light, there is some reason to doubt that any of these men are alive. But there is no doubt that they are unaccounted for. Therefore, we cannot call them dead. Furthermore, even if some—or all—of them are alive, we have a problem in effecting their return. In the past, Communists have been reluctant to release captives they have held illegally and used politically because the captives might have acquired an embarrassing knowledge of Communist methods. Needless to say, however, the Army, working through the agency of the State Department, is continuing to do everything it can to clear up the status of these two hundred and forty-four Army men who remain unaccounted for."

VII

The Wang Report

The Process of Indoctrination—Differences Between North Korean and Chinese Prisoner Handling—The Wang Report

General Trudeau's explanation had given me a fairly clear idea of how the Army prisoner-of-war study had been set up. I next wanted to find out what the service had learned about the two processes—indoctrination and interrogation —that were the main techniques used by the Communists to undermine our soldiers' allegiance to their country. For this information I went to Colonel Willis A. Perry, at that time G-2's Deputy Assistant Chief of Staff for Zone of the Interior Operations, the section charged with security matters; he is now a brigadier general serving in California. I asked Colonel Perry about indoctrination first.

"Indoctrination was an extremely complex process," Colonel Perry told me. "It started to be used only after the Chinese entered the war in November, 1950. Often it began at the very moment of capture. The beginning would

86

be like this. The Chinese to our great bewilderment would greet each captive with a smile, a cigarette, and a handshake. This was a policy for which we were not prepared, and our men without exception were surprised at this maneuver. They had expected to be shot. They had good reason for this assumption. In the first five months of the war, North Koreans had often shot soldiers they could have taken prisoner, or had shot prisoners while combat conditions still existed in the immediate area, simply because they did not want to bother with them. They were completely unprepared, on the whole, to handle prisoners. They had little food to give them, and what there was was often bad; and they had no place to put them. During those early months, the North Koreans would parade the prisoners they did take alive through the streets of their towns in triumph, and then, not knowing quite what to do with them, would herd them into temporary holding camps, where the living conditions varied from poor to dreadful, rather than evacuate them to permanent establishments far behind the lines—a tactic that resulted in many of what the Army calls well-documented combat-type atrocities."

When the United Nations troops were advancing, as they were through most of the fall of 1950, and the North Koreans took prisoners, the Communists often were either unwilling or unable to take them on the retreat with them. Our armies later came upon bodies of prisoners who had been murdered, their hands tied behind them, bullet holes through their heads. "Not a method of handling prisoners,

87

not brainwashing, not even indoctrination or an effort to secure collaboration—just an atrocity," said Perry. According to Army figures, 1,036 of its men were victims of such atrocities after they were taken prisoner but before they reached the prison camps. Word of this naturally spread through the United States ranks, and the men generally came to expect atrocities if they were captured.

But when the Chinese entered the war, they did know how to handle prisoners. They did not ordinarily kill them, no matter what the combat situation, and, in fact, from captured documents we know that Chinese field commanders were told expressly to guard prisoners and try to create a feeling in all of them that China had a "lenient" policy toward "liberated" soldiers. This attitude was in direct contradiction to the attitude of the North Koreans; and to be handed a cigarette instead of the expected bullet in the head, confused our men.

"In a sense, it was the fault of the Army training program that men were sent into combat in Korea without being told that they might expect treatment other than that of the North Koreans upon capture," Perry said. "When a Chinese came up to one our soldiers and offered a handclasp, the American was completely unprepared. It put him off balance. Right then and there, the process of indoctrination began. If the prisoner had been armed with the knowledge that this might happen, its effect might have been very different."

Before describing the Communists' indoctrination technique in Korea any further, Perry suggested I read what he referred to as the Wang Report. This document, some seventy mimeographed pages long, described basic Communist techniques that had been used in China and that were later altered for indoctrination of our GI's. The report was composed of material obtained in a series of interviews a United States government agent had conducted in August, 1953, in a United Nations prisoner-of-war camp on Cheju-do, a South Korean island, with Wang Tsun-ming, an anti-Communist Chinese prisoner of war, then twenty-seven years old. Wang had been a military and counterintelligence officer with the Chinese Nationalist armies on the mainland for four years before being captured by the Communists in 1950 in the civil war in China. For almost a year, he was forcibly re-educated. Ostensibly, he embraced the Communist cause, and was then sent as a private to Korea, where he crossed no-man's-land and surrendered to our forces in the spring of 1951. He is now with Chiang Kai-shek on Formosa.

Described in the report as a natural leader and a man of vigorous action, Wang, through his work as a counter-intelligence officer in the Chinese Nationalist Army, had been able to closely observe Communist methods for seizing and consolidating power over communities and over groups of people. This was in the 1940's, when the conflict on the mainland of China was in a state of flux, and control of an area might pass from the Nationalists to the Communists and back again several times within the space of a couple of years. On retaking an area, each side tried to undo the behind-the-lines successes of the other. Wang's first-hand observations of Communist techniques are, it seems to me, of interest to all of us.

When the Communists became undisputed masters of a village, Wang told his interviewer, the process of Communizing it took eight months or more. In the first phase, which lasted three months, all was sweetness and light. No unpleasant action was taken, and everything that the Communists did appeared to be open and aboveboard. Their slogans were easily understood, and they gave simple explanations for doing things differently from the way that they had been done. Their soldiers were friendly with the people, and sometimes even helped with the farm work. Many of the Chinese became converts to Communism in this early stage because it seemed such a good, peaceful way of life. What the Communists were actually doing during this period, however, was investigating quietly, finding out everything there was to be known about everyone in the town and the surrounding countryside and their relations with one another. When they had learned all they needed to know, the Communists started to organize the local government. They brought together the town's riffraff, the destitute, and the petty thieves, and called them the "progressive" elements. They told them that they were to purge the wealthy class and become the town's rulers. A town meeting was then called and the so-called "progressives" were planted here and there in the gathering, primed to air their grievances against the well-to-do. Certain wealthy individuals were called to account for their exploitation of the people, and were forced, before the meeting, to confess their crimes, real or imaginary. But no matter what they said or what crimes they owned to—even ones they had never committed—their confessions were not satisfactory to the "progressives," who kicked them and beat them, and then accused others in the audience, until that particular meeting ended. That was only the beginning. Next the Communists organized the poor farmers outside the town, and ordered them to accuse the rich farmers, and act in a similar way toward them, at another meeting. Then they mobilized the middle-class farmers to purge the riffraff—who were, you recall, the first "progressives"—by exposing the crimes they had committed before the Communists' arrival, crimes that were, of course, well-known to everybody in the locality.

The Communists were so completely a revolutionary party, Wang pointed out in his report, that their technique for gaining power and consolidating their gains always involved creating complete and utter chaos. They were not satisfied with turning class against class; they went inside each class, even inside each family, to turn individuals against each other and so loosen irreparably the cement that held together the class itself. They sought to break up marital relationships by organizing the wives into various women's groups, thus setting them against their husbands. They tried to create dissension among brothers by exploiting the natural rivalry that always exists. They persuaded grown sons to denounce their parents as reactionaries; and children were singled out for special praise if they informed on their parents. Old-fashioned Chinese, for whom filial piety is one of the highest virtues, were arrested on evidence supplied by their own children, or were struck by them publicly at meetings especially arranged to show the populace that the accepted ideas of the past were not to be tolerated in the new Communist future. Actions like these would have been completely unthinkable to any Chinese before the advent of Communism; but the Communists were able to put them into practice. As the confusion mounted, no one knowing where to turn or how to escape, the Communists ordered the execution of those who had been denounced. The benevolent social order of the first three months had turned into a ravening monster.

After the landlords and rich farmers were purged, and their holdings confiscated, the land was redistributed, the choicest acreage being given by the Communists to those they thought would be most useful to their cause. But the new landholders had no real security, for the purging and confiscating continued as and when it was thought desirable. The reasons given for confiscation were often ridiculous. In one case Wang told of, a farmer was accused by another farmer of stealing an egg. Actually, it developed, the egg had been stolen by the great-grandfather of the accused. The original egg had become a chicken, said the accuser before the public assembly with a straight face; that chicken had produced many more eggs which, in turn, had produced chickens. Therefore the farmer should be fined for his exploitation of all these descendants of the original stolen egg. The bewildered farmer, not really knowing whether the charge was right or wrong, confessed to his great-grandfather's crime. As a fine, the assembly confiscated his farm. By such devices, the Communists were able to take away much of an accused person's property in payment of his—or his ancestors'—alleged exploitations of others. The fines were usually levied by vote in the assembly; and if, after a man had been stripped of all his possessions, he was required to pay still more, he would be told to borrow the balance from friends and relatives.

When the Communists wanted particularly to get rid of a man, the final stage was to force a confession from him before the assembly. This confession would be rejected on the grounds that the man was a chronic liar, that his guilt had been established, and that the reactionary elements in his character could not be changed. An agitator would cry out that the man should be beaten to death. "Progressives" planted about the assembly hall would respond and agree. Sometimes all the members of the assembly would be forced to participate in the execution. Each person would be given a bamboo stick, and they would parade by the victim in single file and give him a blow until he was whipped to death. Thus his blood would be on the hands of every man in the community, and sometimes even of the women and children, since all families in the area were made to take part in these executions. Because they shared this guilt, they were bound to each other and to Communism by a common stigma of blame.

The indoctrination of Army prisoners reflected many aspects of the Wang report, Colonel Perry told me. The principles used to undermine and weaken our men and their relationships were basically the same as those used in China except that psychological pressures replaced the physical ones. The Chinese were solely responsible for this process, and worked without assistance from the North Koreans.

Like the Communist soldiers of the Wang Report, who were so kind to the citizens in a captured area for the first three months, the Chinese holding our men made every effort to appear humane to them in the beginning. After they had shaken their hands and offered them cigarettes, they congratulated them on being released from capitalist bondage. They repeated simple, easily understood slogans, such as "Be a fighter for peace," to them. A prisoner who was hesitant about cooperating was approached with the following plea: "Are you for peace? Of course you are. Every intelligent person is. Then, naturally, you will fight for peace. Good! You are henceforth a true fighter in the cause for peace. Now you will have an opportunity to display the courage of your convictions and fight for peace." The prisoner was then asked to sign a "peace" appeal. If he balked, he was told that by signing he would simply be reaffirming a universal desire of all thinking human beings. Naturally, he wavered in his resistance. It seemed like such a plausible request. And the Communists explained that they wanted him to sign one peace appeal only.

"But the unfortunate thing," said Perry "was that our American prisoners did not understand that to yield once to the Communists was to yield forever. Although many prisoners were promised relief from further requests if they collaborated only once, there is no record of a single case of anyone getting such relief. Once a man started collaborating, he had exactly as much chance of being left alone as the poor Chinese farmer who 'confessed' that his great-grandfather had stolen an egg. But our men did not realize this. They had never met people like the Communists before. In prison camp, our men were faced for the first time with a civilization based completely on the technique of the lie. They often yielded, and were mastered by this lie through ignorance of it and its techniques."

During the initial friendly period, continued the Colonel, the Chinese undertook to find out everything they could about the captives for use in the later indoctrination period, just as they had done with their own people in China. The prisoner was ordered to complete a detailed questionnaire on a sheet of paper with a false heading of the International Red Cross. He was told that the information on it was needed so that the Chinese Red Cross could inform his next of kin that he was a captive. The questions covered his father's occupation, the family's annual income, his own educational background, and other queries that would allow the Chinese to get a line on his socio-economic status. After the first questionnaire, others were issued, progressively more detailed. Later, the prisoners were asked to write autobiographies. Some wrote as many as three; others many more. These enabled the Chinese to pick out the most promising candidates for indoctrination. A captured document of which Colonel Perry showed me a translation gave me an insight into the Communists' thinking: "The prisoners most cooperative in working with us will chiefly be young enlisted men of higher quality," it stated. "They will accept our way of thinking and have the courage to speak and speak actively. We should do our best to encourage and train this type of prisoner and give them due consideration in order to make them work for us and supply us with information. We may ask them to write about the subjects we present to them, but in their own way. In this way, they are allowed to express themselves freely and more information can be obtained."

"The resemblance to the Wang report is plain," said Perry. "Influence the young. This is a cardinal policy of Communism. In China, a premium was placed upon the cooperation of the children; among the prisoners, it was the young enlisted men—the nearest thing in the Army to children—whose collaboration was most actively sought." From the autobiographies, enemy intelligence officers extracted bits of information that might mark the writer as especially susceptible to some aspect of Communism—a Negro's allusion to racial discrimination in the United States, or an account of family financial struggles by a white soldier whose father was a poor coal miner—and these matters were invariably brought up later in indoctrination or interrogation sessions.

VIII

The Life of a Prisoner

Russian Help in Indoctrination—English-Speaking Interrogators and Political Instructors of Chinese Communist Forces—"Mind-conditioning" and "Suction" Phases of Indoctrination

The entire prisoner-indoctrination program of the Chinese, Colonel Perry told me, was inspired, directed, and in some ways assisted, by the Russians. Thousands of Austrians and Germans had been taken prisoner by the Russians in the Second World War, and were subjected to intensive questioning about their knowledge of life in America. Anything they might have gleaned from visiting America, from relatives living there, or from their own schooling was taken down. This information was passed along to the Chinese for use in dealing with Americans.

The Russians are the masters, and, as a matter of fact, the originators, of the prisoner-of-war indoctrination process. It is an adaptation of the severe technique employed by them to extract cooperation and confessions from political prisoners, a phenomenon which was first noticed by the

97

outside world during the Moscow Trials of the 1930's. Prisoner-of-war indoctrination started on the Eastern Front in World War II, nine years before the conflict in Korea. In October, 1941, the Red Army sent a directive to all its interrogators which stated in part, "From the very moment of capture by the Red Army, and during the entire period of captivity, the enemy enlisted men and officers must be under continuous indoctrination by our political workers and interrogators." This directive was followed by others, explaining what type of information should be gathered.

Analysis of these directives show the Communists were then more interested in nonmilitary than military matters, although the latter, of course, were not disregarded. Shortly after capture, the prisoner received a questionnaire of about 140 questions, one of the main purposes of which was to determine his susceptibility to Communist influence. A second questionnaire, provided after reaching a permanent camp, requested very detailed knowledge of the prisoner's political beliefs, his income, his education, his friends and associates in civilian life, and their political beliefs. It also asked for extensive information about the prisoner's family, all his known relatives and their political beliefs and economic status. From this second questionnaire, the Chinese developed data used in the Korean War. On the basis of answers to these two questionnaires, the Russians started an indoctrination program whose purposes were to undermine the faith of the prisoner in his country, and, if possible, to convert him to Communism.

In Korea, the Chinese indoctrination period was marked by the formation of "The Central Peace Committee," the broadcasting of radio propaganda, and the sending of written messages to families and United States troops at the front. In Russia, nearly a decade earlier, the indoctrination had been marked by the establishment of "The German Liberation Committee," the broadcasting of radio propaganda, and the writing of messages to German troops. The patterns, as can be seen, are identical. And the similarity of the patterns is not coincidental.

The Russians, on the basis of their previous experience in handling foreign prisoners, Colonel Perry told me, strongly advised the Chinese to master American ways in order to master Americans. The Chinese followed this advice wholeheartedly. Usually, their interrogators had been educated in the United States. All of them had good backgrounds in American history and geography, and understood our political and economic systems thoroughly. They had access to the latest newspapers, magazines, and books published in this country, and even listened to our radio programs. Their information about current American life was extensive, and they used it adeptly in discussions with the prisoners. They had studied regional American customs, and were able to talk familiarly with men from almost every section of the country, telling them the things that they wanted to hear. They knew the situation among the various races, and could echo the opinions of prisoners belonging to each racial group. They were often so conversant with

99

American slang, and so knowledgeable about Stan Musial's batting average or the landmarks along U. S. Highway No. 1, that many of them might have just got off a plane from the States.

In attempting to indoctrinate our men, the Chinese made no real effort to hide the hand that actually was pulling the strings. They always gave Russia pre-eminence in their political lectures, and it was no accident that the prisoners' articles in camp papers or in peace appeals coupled the glories of China and Russia. The kind of information sought by Chinese military intelligence personnel, and the use to which they put it, make it clear that these officers were an integral part of the Communist propaganda machine, and that the details gained in their interrogation of prisoners were used not so much for military purposes as to further their campaign of subverting the prisoners' loyalty and of influencing the free world.

Planned, serious, and intensive indoctrination was begun in the first permanent prison camp in North Korea in March, 1951. It spread to other camps as they were established along the Manchurian border. These camps were administered by a military as well as a political section, both under the supervision of a camp commander, whom the prisoners rarely saw. As a general rule, the prisoners also had little to do with the non-English-speaking Chinese in the military division, who were responsible for guarding them. The Chinese who were most important to them were the English-speaking interrogators and the political instructors.

These two groups of men formed a distinctive element in the Chinese Communist armed forces. Their backgrounds were predominantly civilian, and they looked like civilians, despite the standard Chinese uniforms they wore. They all spoke English, which many of them had learned, they said, from years spent attending various colleges in the United States; though their skill with the language ranged from fluent and colloquial to stilted, they could always get their meaning across to the prisoners, even when they sounded like textbooks. Whether in a classroom conducting a personal interrogation, or in a self-criticism session, the efforts of these men were spent entirely on making Communist doctrine clear. They enjoyed a favored status in the Chinese military hierarchy, being burdened with little or no routine command responsibility. In age, they ranged from twenty to forty-five.

To the prisoners, the more important of the two groups were the political instructors. Each instructor had the power to order or remit punishment, to facilitate a man's going on sick call, to lighten camp duties or make them more burdensome. His position combined many of the functions that our Army delegates to the Information and Education Branch, the Inspector General's Office, the Chaplain's Branch, and Special Services. The political instructor was chiefly responsible for the subversion of our men's loyalties.

"The indoctrination of prisoners of war in a prison camp is, of course, a somewhat different process from Communizing an area on the mainland of China," said Perry.

"In China, the Communists were seeking to purge reactionary elements and to redistribute the land; in the prison camps, their goals were to isolate reactionaries and redistribute ideas. Indoctrination involves much less force than outright compulsory Communization, because the process of indoctrination aims at making converts through apparent kindness or, at the very worst, through strong psychological pressures. The Communists did not want to kill our men. Ideally they wanted to turn them into evangelists—have them accept espionage missions and come back to the United States prepared to spread the Communist word, covertly or openly, among our citizens. They could not obtain these results with beatings, torture, and death. Besides defeating their own purpose in a long-range sense, such tactics would have created a short-range problem in prisoner control. If the Communists had tortured or killed our men, their buddies would have banded together in a unified way to resist their captors. Therefore, force was kept at a minimum in the Chinese handling of our men, although stiff psychological pressures were applied whenever necessary."

The organization of the permanent camps was simple. The chief prisoner units were the companies. They ranged in number in various camps from three to seven, and in size from 60 to 350 prisoners. The average company contained about 200 men. It was divided into three or four platoons which, in turn, were divided into squads of 6 to 15 prisoners; most of the camp routine revolved about this lowest unit. During indoctrination the members of the progressive squads attended classes, studied, and held their discussions together.

On an average day in one of the camps, the Colonel told me, the prisoners' schedule of activities began at seven in the morning. It ended at seven in the evening, when they were bedded down. During the period of indoctrination, five of these twelve hours—from nine in the morning until noon, and from two in the afternoon until four—were spent hearing lectures or attending discussions. In addition, those men who wished more time for study would be excused from bed check until nine o'clock, and might spend these two hours in the camp library. The library was open from six to nine in the evening, and was well-stocked with Communist reading matter in English; an average library held about 150 books. These included Cominform journals, Communist Party publications, and theoretical works by well-known Marxist writers, as well as fiction by such non-Marxists as Tolstoy, Victor Hugo, Dickens, Upton Sinclair, Erskine Caldwell, and John Steinbeck—writers whose depictions of social conditions under capitalism or under a monarchy were apparently acceptable to the Communists. Librarians were usually progressive prisoners, appointed by the Chinese, who were responsible for keeping the library open and clean, and for taking care of the books.

Lectures were usually given in a room in one of the larger buildings; in one camp, they were held in what had been a village schoolhouse before the Communists had removed all the villagers to make room to build the camp. Behind the instructor in each lecture room hung a huge flag showing a white dove of peace on a red ground; above the dove were the English words, "Grand Rally in Support of World Peace." In mild weather, classes were moved out-of-doors.

The indoctrination program was divided into two phases. The first phase was called by Army psychiatrists the "mind-conditioning" phase. During this period, the lectures aimed at making the prisoners hate America. They were told that the South Koreans had treacherously attacked the peaceful North Koreans as a result of machinations between President Truman and Syngman Rhee; that these machinations, in turn, had been instigated by Wall Street capitalists intent on starting a third World War in order to raise prices on the stock market; that the Chinese Communists had come to the aid of North Korea only to thwart the desire of Truman, Rhee, and MacArthur to utilize North Korea as a base for the invasion of Manchuria ("Wouldn't the defense of Mexico by the United States be justified if Chinese forces had been ordered to attack Texas?"); and that the United States, a wretched, backward nation where the Negro was a second-class citizen, had plainly showed, by placing warships in the Straits of Formosa, that it wanted to dominate China through support of the bandit, Chiang Kai-shek.

In the second part of the indoctrination, termed the "suction" phase, the enemy compared the idyllic life of the "new democracies" under Communism to that which had existed in "the old states of reaction." The instructor argued the advantages of living in the China of Mao Tze-tung as against that of Chiang Kai-shek, or of living in the Iron Curtain countries of the present day rather than under the parliaments and kings that had ruled these countries in the past. Prisoners were required to read the writings of Lenin and Stalin and to make extensive notes as an aid to understanding their ideas. The indoctrination process, unfortunately, was greatly helped by the ignorance of the captive GI's, whose formal education on the average had ended with the ninth grade of school. Not only did the prisoners not know much about the history of Communism, they didn't know much about that of the United States either. The following incident shows their ignorance. In the indoctrination lectures, the Communists frequently displayed global charts dotted with our military bases, the names of which were of course known to many of the captives. "See these bases?" the instructor would say, tapping them on the chart with his pointer. "They are American—full of war materiel. You *know* they are American. And you can see they are ringing Russia and China. Russia and China do not have one base outside their own territory. From this it's clear which side is the warmonger. Would America have these bases and spend millions to maintain them were it not preparing to war on Russia and China?" This argument seemed plausible to many of the prisoners. In general they had no idea that these bases showed not the United States' wish for war, but its wish for peace, that they had been established as part of a series of treaties aimed not at conquest, but at curbing Red aggression. Gaps like these in the prisoners' knowledge were unfortunate, and in many cases they counted heavily against us.

The techniques by which the Communists indoctrinated our men were not based on physical force. There is no record in any of the returnees' files of the use of physical force or physical torture *as a means of indoctrination*. The techniques were, rather, wholly psychological, and were three in number: repetition, harassment, and humiliation.

Repetition was used both in classes and in individual instruction. Prisoners were required to memorize certain material, such as the contents of a pamphlet on Communist ideology, and they were examined on this material day in and day out, week in and week out. While they were being crammed with this literature and questioned on it over and again, the prisoners were given no other duties and were allowed to read nothing else. The system proved successful; it hammered into the heads of the men a biased but firm knowledge of Communist principles. Many of these re-educated Americans had immature minds. Some of them had not gone beyond the fifth grade in our schools. But when they returned to the United States, they had acquired a wealth of information about Marxism. They could recite entire passages from memory, and they had studied the theoretical writings of Lenin and Stalin until they could argue the merits of Communism and its superiority to democracy with some of the best educated of the specially trained Army interrogators.

The technique of harassment was equally successful. It was used on all the men; even the most fawning progressives were subjected to it when their captors wished greater cooperation from them. The most minor offense, deliberate or not, could set the technique in motion. Suppose a prisoner failed to answer a question in class. He was ordered to camp headquarters and given a long lecture on the grave necessity of paying strict attention to the instructor and remembering what was said. This was only the beginning. That same prisoner would be called to headquarters again, perhaps at midnight, and lectured in the same way. The next day, he might be in the latrine when he was summoned, in haste, and given another lecture on his grievous shortcomings. Then he would be aroused at two o'clock the next morning, and once again his offenses would be discussed. The Chinese knew that this treatment deprived the prisoners of what they wanted above everything else—to be left alone to lead a normal prisoner's life. The Army study showed that most prisoners felt if they complied with the enemy at the time, they would be left alone thereafter. But they learned, to their sorrow, that this never happened. Harassment continued, and even increased.

Of the three tactics, the third, humiliation, did the most psychological damage. Prisoners were specifically promised, in speeches that Chinese commanders made to them on the battlefield immediately after they were captured, and in literature given them in the camps, that under the "lenient" policy of their captors they would not be subject to humiliation. Despite these promises, prisoners were humiliated whenever the Communists desired. Colonel Perry gave me an example of how humiliation was used. During indoctrination class one day, a prisoner pointed out that if, as the instructor had said, South Korea had started the war, and not North Korea, it was odd that by the end of the first day of combat the North Koreans had not only repelled the treacherous onslaught of the South Koreans all along the front, but were already knocking at the gates of Seoul, forty miles to the south. The instructor was furious. "You are a stupid, ignorant fool," he said. "Everyone else in the class knows the South Koreans started the war. Why don't you?" But the prisoner was obdurate. He demanded an answer, whereupon the instructor ordered the entire class to stand, and remain on its feet until this one man abandoned his objection. After some hours of standing, the other prisoners began to mutter against the objector. Under this pressure the man capitulated. But the incident did not end there. The next day, the prisoner had to compose and read to the class a long criticism of his own conduct, ending with an apology to the class and to the instructor. On each of the following four or five days, he had to repeat his self-criticism and elaborate upon it. His classmates were ordered to criticize him, which they did. Then he, in turn, was made to criticize his classmates. This, as the Wang report showed, is one of the important Communist methods of bringing about chaos in a group's relations. When members of various classes and families in the Chinese village arose in public and proceeded to denounce each other, the eventual result was that no one in the class or family trusted anyone else, not even his own brother. In the prison camp, incidents like this classroom one led to chaos and favored the establishment of an informer system. The step from confessing one's own offenses to informing on one's associates seemed an easy and natural one for an individual to take after he had done enough of the former. The transition, of course, was actively encouraged by the Communists. "You could not rely on anyone," was a comment all too frequently made by returned prisoners.

This lack of trust was debilitating. "One of the primary duties of any Army man who is taken prisoner," said Perry, "is, and always has been, to escape. The informer system effectively thwarted this. During the entire Korean War, there was not a single successful American escape from a permanent prison camp. It was the first war in United States military history of which this can be said."

IX

Interrogation Techniques

The Process of Interrogation—Army Definition of Torture—
Description of Enemy Interrogation Headquarters and Methods

Interrogation was the second of the Communists' two most
important techniques for manipulating our men. It was
used both to gain military information and to assist indoctrination; the Chinese used it mainly for the latter purpose.
Men who were slow to be indoctrinated; men from whom
some specific act of collaboration was wanted, such as the
signing or circulation of peace petitions or the writing or
broadcasting of propaganda messages; or men the Communists were trying to get to inform on their fellow prisoners were all subjected to lengthy and trying sessions of
interrogation. A man might be interrogated over and over
again for weeks until he yielded, or until the Communists
gave up on him.

The internationally accepted standards for handling military captives are embodied in the Articles of the Geneva

Conventions of 1949 Relative to the Treatment of Prisoners of War, more commonly known as the Geneva Convention. Its provisions do not prohibit or limit the questioning of prisoners of war, nor are prisoners themselves forbidden to answer any questions asked. However, Article 17 of the Convention, which states in part, "Every prisoner of war, when questioned on the subject, is bound to give only his surname, first names and rank, date of birth, and army, regimental, personal or serial number, or, failing this, equivalent information," gives prisoners the specific right to refuse to divulge anything beyond these basic facts. Supporting a prisoner's right to keep silence, the Geneva Convention further states, "No physical violence or mental torture, nor any other form of coercion, may be inflicted on prisoners of war to secure from them information of any kind whatever. Prisoners of war who refuse to answer may not be threatened, insulted, or exposed to unpleasant or disadvantageous treatment of any kind."

In direct contradiction to these rules, Communist interrogation almost always made use of coercion. It was, in fact, an essential part of Communist interrogation technique. Prisoners were threatened with nonrepatriation, for instance, if they didn't talk. It was standard procedure for an interrogator to lay a pistol on the table in front of him at the start of each session, to serve as a reminder to the prisoner that if he did not cooperate, he might be shot. Torture was also constantly threatened. The fact is, however, that no prisoners were transported to Manchuria, nor were any shot or tortured if they did not cooperate at interrogations. "The Army defines torture as the application of pain so extreme that it causes a man to faint or lose control of his will," Colonel Perry said to me. "The bastinado, the iron maiden, the rack, water dropping unceasingly on the head, bamboo splinters stuck under the fingernails and ignited—these are forms of torture. The Army does not consider prisoners being made to stand in water, being improperly clad, being kicked, slapped, or kept in cramped quarters as torture. These things are uncomfortable, and they do cause stress. But it is stress of the same general order as a combat soldier undergoes, and a prisoner must be able to endure such stress just as the combat soldier must endure the gunfire and close-quarter lunges of the enemy on the battlefield."

The chief interrogator at each Communist camp, the Colonel said, was a well-educated, polished, expert officer, and a fluent conversationalist in English, as were most of his assistants. The staff of interrogators in a camp usually included two or three Chinese women, who served as assistants to the men and kept records on each prisoner who had been questioned, the results of the interrogation, and the date each man was to return for another session. Their functions were purely administrative. They were not used as lures for the prisoners; the Communists did not permit fraternizing between prisoners and women workers in the camps. Most questioning sessions took place in the interrogation room, usually situated in the camp headquar-

ters building near the office of the commandant. These
rooms were equipped, as our men learned sooner or later,
with various listening and recording devices, and with one-
way-vision mirrors. The room was never closed, the section
operating on a twenty-four-hour basis.

I asked Colonel Perry what returned prisoners had reported about the actual course of an interrogation, and he
gave me an account of what took place when one prisoner
was called in for the first time for questioning. The man
was escorted to the interrogation by a progressive, taken
into the interrogation room by a Chinese staff member, and
seated at a plain table opposite the interrogator. The interrogator announced, at this initial interview, that he
would like first to talk about personal matters. "Now we
visit" was his gambit as he smilingly laid his pistol on the
table.

One of the women assistants brought in a large folder
with the prisoner's name on it, some papers that were sup-
posed to be reports, marked "Secret" and "Top Secret,"
and a stack of United States Army manuals. The interrogator informed the prisoner that the folder contained considerable information about him, and read out his name,
rank, serial number, and perhaps the organization to which
he had been assigned at the time of his capture. He then
closed the folder and took up some of the so-called secret
reports; these, he told the prisoner, had been sent from the
United States by Communist friends, and contained evidence that the American people did not want the war in

Korea to continue and also that the Truman government had aggressive designs on the rest of the world, particularly Russia and China. As the next step the interrogator casually recited a number of facts he already knew about the prisoner's own and other front-line units, and about the United States Army in general. This was to make the prisoner feel that it hardly mattered what he told, since the enemy probably already possessed any information he could reveal. Throughout, the interrogator tried to give the impression that the prisoner himself was of no importance and that he had been summoned to headquarters only as a matter of routine. Meanwhile, although the prisoner thought he was talking with the interrogator in private, in adjoining rooms his words were being recorded, and his reactions were being observed through one-way-vision mirrors.

Interrogation sessions lasted for indefinite periods of time. Some were brief, others were long and trying, and the length of the session did not necessarily depend on the amount of information a prisoner could or would give. The constant aim of the Communists was to keep the prisoners off balance. A prisoner could be released after ten minutes' questioning, only to be summoned again in an hour. Often a prisoner was kept for an unusually long time simply to show others in his hut what might happen to them, and thus, the Chinese theory went, to prevail on them to talk freely so as to be released sooner, when they were called. The interrogator talked harshly to some men in order to create fear, not only in that man—who would then, the

Communists felt, be more likely to cooperate—but also in the other men awaiting interrogation to whom that man would describe his experience. The secret reports were fakes, of course, and the data in the prisoner's personal folder were only fragmentary, consisting usually of the questionnaire filled out by the man himself in his early days in the camp. If the Communists had had the facts they wanted about each man, they would have had no need to question him. However, by a process of constant, repetitive interrogation the information they wanted was often gradually acquired.

After a questioning session, the interrogator would frequently give the prisoner a personal-history form, similar to the one he had been given earlier, and order him to fill it out in detail, in his own words and handwriting. The prisoner was left alone in the interrogation room to complete the paper, having been told to take as long as he liked, meditate, think of everything in his past life, and record it. If the interrogator did not think the result was satisfactory, he would give the form back to the prisoner and tell him to supply additional information. The idea of having a prisoner write his personal history in addition to undergoing interrogation, Perry told me, was unheard of in our military history before the Korean War. The scheme, when it succeeded, provided the Communists with intelligence they could never have obtained from other sources. Some men wrote as many as five hundred pages during their imprisonment, about their lives, their families, their friends, and their relationship with the Army. These statements were kept on file and studied carefully before each interrogation, so that the interrogator could use the autobiographical material as a guide to go deeper at each session into the past life and character of the prisoner. The records on each interrogation, and even of chance remarks dropped in the interrogation room, were used to check the accuracy of each prisoner's written statements about himself, statements made by other prisoners about him, and statements he made about other prisoners. Some prisoners were interrogated as often as fifty times during their captivity. This method of interrogation worked so well that not only did each man supply additional information at almost every session, but also the chances of his sticking to a false, or cover, story were just about ruled out as a practical possibility. "The data from these interrogations, and from the questionnaires and autobiographies that the Chinese collected," Perry said, "represent the largest fund of information about the American soldier ever acquired by an enemy." There is no reason to suppose that the weaknesses and strengths, the gullibilities and insights, of United States military personnel are not at this minute being carefully studied in Peiping and Moscow.

X

Communist Use of the Mails

Communist Handling of Prisoner Mail—Geneva Convention
Violations in General and Those Pertaining to Mail in Particular—Communists' Three Aims in Prisoner Handling

In addition to using the techniques of indoctrination and
interrogation to manipulate captives, the Communists also
made use of a third, less important, but nonetheless effective
maneuver—they manipulated the flow of the prisoners'
mail. I was briefed on this matter by Lieutenant Colonel
Charles M. Trammell, Jr., then, as mentioned earlier, a
plans and policy officer serving as special counsel to G-2;
now he is a civilian working in the Pentagon. Trammell, a
United States Government trial attorney in Michigan when
he was recalled to military service in 1952, was the head of
the group that planned the counterintelligence part of the
questionnaire submitted to returned prisoners and directed
the counterintelligence research phase of the Army study.

The Communists made not the slightest effort, Colonel

Trammell told me, to comply with the Geneva Convention's basic provision about mail. This provision states that every prisoner, as soon as possible following capture, and not more than a week after his arrival at a camp, shall be allowed to write directly to his family, and also to the Central Prisoners of War Agency provided for in Article 123 of the Convention, notifying both of his capture, his whereabouts, and his state of health.

The status of the United States and its adversaries with regard to the Geneva Convention during the Korean War was a peculiar one. Through a legislative fluke, this country had not signed the 1949 agreement, then and now the pertinent document. For other reasons, neither had the North Korean or Chinese Communist governments. Since the war we have signed the 1949 agreement, and the other two governments, although not actual signatories, have by recent acts of accession agreed, with certain reservations, to follow it.

Despite this country's lack of technical ratification at the time of the war, we nevertheless scrupulously followed the convention's provisions. Communist prison-camp commanders, however, sometimes said they were and sometimes said they were not following the policies of the convention, depending on which position suited their convenience at the moment. In either case, scant attention was paid to provisions that church attendance be permitted, that the dead be buried with the words of committal used in the religion of the deceased, and that members of the International Red Cross be allowed to make regular visits to the camps. "These were but a few Communist violations of the convention," Trammell said. "There would be no use to catalogue them all now, but an interesting official dossier could sometime be made on them."

The Communist handling of mail was just one of a number of violations, but clearly expressed the Communist attitude toward the entire convention. The convention lists letters as the approved way for prisoners to communicate with home; instead the Communists urged them to communicate with their families by making propaganda broadcasts—a typical example of the way they turned the compassionate provisions of the convention to their own purposes. The convention also provides that prisoners shall be authorized to send telegrams to their homes in cases of emergency, or when they have been without news for a long period. The messages are to be charged against their accounts with their captors or paid for with currency at their disposal. The Communists permitted no telegrams like these, however many cases of emergency arose among the prisoners and despite the fact that many of them were without news for long periods. Instead, the only telegrams allowed to be sent by the prisoners were Communist-inspired propaganda messages in the form of peace petitions.

The convention, which specifically notes that prisoners are allowed to send and receive letters and cards, further states that these must be conveyed by the most rapid means at the disposal of the captors, and never intercepted or delayed for disciplinary reasons. In Korea, however, mail was delivered to the prisoners only at highly irregular intervals. One prisoner stated that of the 125 letters he received in three years of captivity, 54 were delivered at one time and 26 within the following month. Most letters received, including those sent by airmail which should have arrived in ten days at the most, took from two to six months to reach the prisoners. As for outgoing mail, only a small fraction of the letters written by prisoners ever reached their destination. One prisoner learned on his return that of the 150 letters he had sent, only twenty-six were ever delivered. The likelihood of a letter's reaching its destination increased proportionately with the amount of material it contained that was favorable to the Communists. Almost all the letters that reached the United States did, in fact, contain propaganda of some sort, and those addressed to important persons or to large organizations with wide public influence were given priority over those to lesser persons, including the families of soldiers. As to what became of the letters that did not arrive, there may be some clue in the reports made by a number of prisoners who had been sent out together on a work detail; these men said they came upon several hundred letters from prisoners dumped in a drainage ditch by the side of the road.

"Of course, the Communists did nothing so crude as to admit they were withholding or destroying mail," Trammell said. "But it was noticeable that many of the prisoners who cooperated received their mail from home relatively quickly.

In Communist hands, mail was an instrument of persuasion, and as the knowledge that it was being used in this way spread among the men, the power of the weapon increased. Mail was never processed in the ordinary way; in fact, it was used purely and simply to manipulate prisoners. Letters from home help the morale of prisoners in many ways, not the least being that they are tangible evidence of the memories, hopes, and concerns the prisoner shares with those at home. It suited the Communists' purposes exactly to disrupt this communication, thus isolating each prisoner and making him feel insecure by breaking his ties with home. This was done subtly, of course; the line was not completely severed, but the letters were thoroughly screened. Those that would most disrupt a man's peace of mind—the complaining letters or the depressing ones—were let through. Since the prisoner was bound to feel that any complaint from someone safe and free in the United States was wholly unreasonable, this kind of screening was very effective."

Mail was not censored in the usual way, Trammell said; that is, no phrases were cut out of letters—which lulled prisoners into believing there was no censorship. Instead, if the contents of a letter did not suit Communist purposes, the entire letter was simply destroyed. Prisoners who complained about a lack of mail were given routine answers, none so farfetched as to sound unreasonable. One answer was that mail that had reached North Korea had been destroyed by United States bombing raids; another was that Americans were too busy with their own affairs to write; a third, that the United States Army had not forwarded any letters. If a prisoner complained frequently, or if it was obvious that he was disturbed over lack of mail, a "friendly" Communist would have a chat with him about his problem, offer to investigate, and later hand over a few letters, thus creating in him a sense of gratitude. To many of the prisoners, in their isolated situation, the explanations for the dearth of mail seemed logical; and some of them began to feel bitter toward the United States Army and toward the Air Force for "bombing" mail, perhaps even bitter toward their families for not writing. The Communists so successfully destroyed the faith of some prisoners in America by their manipulation of mail that these men wrote hostile letters to their families in which they said how grateful they were to the Communists for trying to help them get mail that the United States Army was preventing from reaching them.

As for other mail, such as newspapers, magazines, books, and packages, not a single item in these categories was ever received by a prisoner in any known instance, Trammell said. Articles of this kind were sent freely from America throughout the war by relatives, are permitted prisoners by the Geneva Convention, and were, of course, received in other wars.

As additional violations of the convention principles governing mail, the Communists screened outgoing letters for use in radio propaganda broadcasts and also made photostatic copies of those letters considered sufficiently disruptive of morale to be suitable for airdrop to United States troops fighting at the front. One prisoner, Master Sergeant Artesani, discovered quite by chance that his mail was being used for propaganda purposes in this way. In 1952, a newly-captured prisoner in his camp showed him a photostatic copy of a letter that Artesani had written earlier to his wife. In it Artesani had said, not unnaturally, that he missed his daughter and that he wished he could see her. It was a letter full of a father's natural yearning for his child. To make Artesani's plight more poignant, and their propaganda more effective, the Communists had attached to the photostat of the letter a picture of a child that Artesani had never seen before. "When he went indignantly, photostat in hand, to camp authorities to protest such an illegal use of his mail, he was told by his captors that they could and would use any letter in any way that they felt appropriate without any consideration of its author," Trammell said.

As a result of its study, the Army has concluded that the techniques of indoctrination, interrogation, and this kind of mail-handling were part of a well-planned Communist program which had three aims. First, the program sought to disseminate propaganda favorable to Communism and unfavorable to the West across the world, particularly in the critical areas in Asia and Africa. Second, it sought to control prisoners with a minimum of difficulty and a minimum use of guards. Third, it sought the outright conversion of our men to Communism—or, failing that, at least their acquiescence to the possible rightness of the Communist position.

The Army believes that this program succeeded in achieving its first two aims. Propaganda was made and was successfully disseminated; prisoners were controlled with a minimum of effort. The Army feels reasonably doubtful about their achievement of the third aim. However, it will take some time before it can be determined the extent to which individual prisoners accepted or rejected Communism, and whether their loyalty to their own country was weakened or strengthened by the experiences they underwent in enemy prison camps.

XI

Reactionaries and Progressives

Army Statement of Difference Between Brainwashing and Indoctrination—Prisoners Divided Into Categories by Psychiatrist —Under Communism, System Only Source of Praise or Blame

The treatment American prisoners underwent at the hands of the Communists cannot, the Army believes, be called "brainwashing." "Brainwashing," as defined by the Army, is a process producing obvious alteration of character. However the alteration is accomplished—whether by hypnosis, drugs, physical torture, extreme psychological pressures, or some combination of these—the subject clearly ceases to be the person he was before. According to the repatriates' own accounts, the kind of severe measures required to effect a personality change were not employed at any time with Army prisoners.

The Army opinion on this subject was given me by Major Harry A. Segal, at the time of our talk a psychiatrist in the Army Medical Corps. Major Segal was Chief of the

Neuropsychiatric Consultation Service at Walter Reed Hospital and, before that had been head of the psychiatric personnel of the ten Joint Intelligence Processing Teams that had handled the repatriation of Korean prisoners; the Army felt he knew a great deal about the psychological aspects of the enemy program and more than anyone else in its organization about the psychological condition of the returned prisoners. He had personally conducted psychiatric interviews with eighty returned prisoners; he had later studied the files of 800 men in an attempt to identify possible emotional factors which might have produced collaborators, or, on the other hand, resisters; and he had supervised the psychiatric evaluations of approximately 1400 prisoners who even remotely seemed possible candidates for hospital treatment. He is now engaged in private practice in Washington, D. C.

Any process severe enough to have produced character alteration, Major Segal told me, would have been in direct conflict with the avowedly "lenient" policy of the Chinese. In addition, severity could not have been used in dealing with the men without arousing resentment and even rebellion among them, which was exactly what the Chinese policy aimed at avoiding. That their policy was highly successful in avoiding resentment is obvious from the extensive incidence of American prisoners' fraternization with the Chinese enemy. This fraternization was in marked contrast to the hatred felt by American prisoners toward their Japanese captors in the Second World War, and was a direct result of the difference between Chinese and Japanese policies. The Japanese, who wanted no Americans in their Far East Co-prosperity Sphere, treated their captives with such harshness that the prisoners banded solidly together against them. The Chinese, on the other hand, made pretensions of leniency, and used psychology to control the prisoners' resentment by transferring it to objects other than their captors. The anger of a prisoner who had yielded was, more often than not, ultimately turned back against himself, while his captors, in his eyes, remained blameless. Many returned prisoners, for example, said that the Chinese had treated them "as well as they could," and they even expressed sincere gratitude for the care they had received, in spite of the fact that the conditions under which they were kept were far worse than anything they had ever known. When they talked about politics, they often used the term "Socialism" rather than "Communism," and said that while Socialism might not work in the United States where people are for the most part well-off to begin with, it was a good thing for China and other less advanced nations since under it the downtrodden lower classes are able to improve their lot—thus showing a significant emotional and intellectual identification with the Communist point of view.

The technique which the enemy used on the American prisoners has been called by the Army, *indoctrination;* a general definition of this process was given earlier. Through indoctrination, Major Segal explained, collaboration was obtained by taking advantage of a man's weakest character points. If the man seemed the type who would give in to harassment or threats, he was harassed or threatened. If he might respond to flattery and reward, he was flattered or rewarded. The rewards were small, Segal said; and the degree to which they were increased never matched the growth of the demands made upon the man who yielded in the hope of reward. The collaborator was never paid in full.

Psychologically, the prisoners fell into six categories. Three of these categories came under the general heading of outright collaborator; all told about 13 per cent of the captives fell in this category. Under this heading, Segal said, were, first of all, men with little capacity for enduring stress, who capitulated early in the game. (The reaction to stress was invariably a highly individual and personal matter. One of the most notorious collaborators, by his own admission, gave information to the Communists after no more than thirty-five minutes of not very intensive questioning. "They said they had ways of making me talk, so I talked," he explained on his return. Another man, despite every effort the Communists could make, said nothing throughout his three years of captivity. "I was told not to communicate with the enemy, so I didn't," he said.) Prisoners in this first group lacked the moral stamina to resist even minimal emotional discomfort. They were, in effect, cowards; there seems to be no other word in ordinary language appropriate to them.

The second group of collaborators might be labelled opportunists. They yielded for strictly personal and selfish reasons. They were the sort who would inform, sign petitions, and make broadcasts because for this they would receive tangible benefits—freedom to walk outside the camp compound, an egg or two, cigarettes. "They were also given power over the other men, prestige, and the approval of their captors—very important rewards, psychologically, to such individuals," said Segal. "During a psychiatric interview, one of them described his ability to expound Communist doctrine. 'The Communists told me I was a young Lenin,' he said. And, as he remembered this, his face lit up." Despite their acts of collaboration, these men appeared to have no deep-seated convictions about Communism or any real understanding of its techniques. Interestingly enough, after their release many tried to continue in the role of informer, approaching high-level officers in our own Army with offers to give information about other repatriates.

The third, and smallest, group of collaborators consisted of those who actually accepted Communism. In general, the men who took this step seemed to be those who for various reasons had been unable to form any strong attachments or loyalties in their past lives. "The simplest way to define this group," said Segal, "would be to say that they were the kind of men who say to themselves, 'I'm just a kid. I don't know where I'm going. I don't know whether people actually like me. Will I ever really be a success?' Because they were uncertain of themselves and unsatisfied with what they had been so far, they were willing to become part of a system as different as possible from the one that had proved unsatisfactory for them."

The fourth category, and the one that included the overwhelming majority of the prisoners—three out of four, that is—was made up of men who chose what seemed to them to be the path of least resistance. Group discipline was sadly missing in the prison camps. Lacking this discipline, which would have shielded them all from harassment, the men in this class tried to substitute a form of protection of their own making. They complied outwardly with the less extreme demands made by the Communists. The petitions they signed and the broadcasts they made were relatively harmless. They cooperated in indoctrination and interrogation sessions in a passive sort of way, although there was a tendency to refuse to do anything obviously traitorous. Among the prisoners themselves, this outward compliance was known as "playing it cool."

In their examination of the returned prisoners, the Army psychiatrists tried to find out whether hereditary or environmental factors might have had anything to do with a man's either collaborating or resisting. Segal and some others selected 805 men (a random sample from the nearly 3,400 repatriates), and divided them into four sections of about 200 each. They gave each section intelligence tests, had them fill out sociological and personality questionnaires, and tested their attitudes according to a scale based on studies in human attitudes and values made at the University of California. Nothing could be found in the 805 men's heredity, environment, rearing, education, family background, occupation, race, or religion that explained their good or poor conduct as prisoners. Resisters as well as collaborators were scattered throughout every category that could be devised, and no significant correlations could be discerned.

Of course, in this study of the 805 men, as Segal pointed out to me, there were many imponderables to be considered. One of the important factors, for instance, was the relationship between the captive and his political instructor. Some of the instructors were described as dull robots, others as zealous fanatics. "The matter of an instructor's personal enthusiasm and his quickness to respond to the subject's interests and the subject's mental shifts, was, naturally, a very potent factor in influencing a subject's conduct, whether the subject was aware of it or not," Segal said. "For instance, one of the returnees told me, 'My political instructor helped me a lot. I talked my family problems over with him, and he was sort of a father confessor. When I get home, I'm going to act exactly like he said.' This soldier had been having trouble with his wife on the one hand, and his mother and mother-in-law on the other. Another instructor might have wielded no power over him whatever. But this particular instructor did. Unravelling the psychology of a prisoner's acts is unquestionably tied up with this complicated link—to which we still don't have the key."

Reactionaries were divided into two groups, the total number in both being roughly equivalent to the total number of frank collaborators, or about 13 per cent. Reactionaries were those men who never gave the Communists any information beyond their name, rank, serial number, and date of birth; who refused to write their autobiography; and who refused to give the information contained in Army field manuals even after the Communist interrogator held the books up before them and said, "Look, we already have it." Some of these men even refused to give the enemy the four permissible items of information.

The first group of reactionaries included individuals with a long history of unwillingness to accept any kind of authority. They had bad behavior records in our own Army, and in prison camp they merely persisted in their old pattern of rebelling against those in command. As resisters, they were not effective; men like these would bullheadedly set fire to a barracks even though the whole camp would have to pay for the act. The other group of reactionaries were mature, well-integrated individuals who knew how to use their intelligence constructively, how to work with all sorts of men, and how to influence them to gain a goal of importance to them all, how to use the respect they had earned from other prisoners to quietly sabotage the indoctrination program. "These men were the true heroes of the prison camps," said Segal. "They were manly enough to refuse to submit to indoctrination and accept favors from the Communists, and they maintained their integrity and personal honor throughout their captivity."

When the indoctrination program got under way, the

reactionaries were usually segregated in units within the camps, or were sent to other camps where reactionaries predominated. In these latter camps little or no indoctrination was tried. Reactionaries were described by the Communists to the other prisoners as "ignorant, stubborn, professional soldiers." They were given hard-labor details, but otherwise they were left alone. The hard labor benefited the reactionaries, for it kept them busy, often improved their health, and gave them a better mental outlook for facing the serious problems of confinement.

In the so-called progressive camps, the Chinese instituted a full-scale indoctrination program for the progressives. These men were given little physical work to do, and were never left to themselves, but were always being urged to study. The emphasis was all on re-education; and often boredom at having nothing better to do than to read Communist textbooks drove the progressive to do exactly as his captors wished and become interested in what he was studying.

I asked Colonel Perry whether the Army, using the data available on personnel sheets, had been able to differentiate between progressive and reactionary units. He said it had been impossible to do this with much exactness. Each group included men of all ages, with many different educational, economic, and military backgrounds—senior officers and nonsenior enlisted men, men who had college degrees and those whose schooling had stopped with the fifth grade. However, he did add that the greatest number of men in the progressive category were between the ages of eighteen and twenty-four; were usually, although not always, of superior intelligence but without much formal education, or social or political maturity; and that most of them had their origins in this country in lower-income groups which were indiscriminately rural and urban.

I asked if the reactionaries had been made to suffer for their resistance to the Communists. Colonel Perry answered no, that the Army study showed that the death rate among reactionaries was little, if any, higher than among collaborators. The Chinese took captive one American who had run out of ammunition, the Colonel said. They proceeded to ask him his opinion of General George C. Marshall. "General George C. Marshall is a great American soldier," he replied, and a rifle butt knocked him to the ground. The question was repeated. So was his answer. But this time he wasn't knocked down. He had won his battle. The Communists were testing his resistance, and had found out what sort of man he was. They respected him for his attitude, and he was not struck again. After three years in prison camp, during which he unwaveringly rejected everything the Communists stood for, he was repatriated, his principles intact. Another prisoner, who also refused to yield, said of this man, "He had been willing to sacrifice his life on the battlefield. And after his capture he was still willing to sacrifice it. In following to the best of his ability the course that seemed to him morally correct for all Americans, he was willing to suffer. He was willing to die."

In contrast to this is a story Colonel Perry told me of a private first class who yielded to the Communists, absorbed their point of view along with a lot of half-digested economic theories, and helped their propaganda campaign by writing articles for the newspaper put out by collaborators in his prison camp. The following, entitled "A Wised-Up G.I.," is one of his articles, which the Colonel permitted me to copy:

My name is ——— ———, I've been in the army seven months, and I'm glad that I'm one of the liberated G.I.'s because I've learned how my government has tricked me and my friends and family.

Fellows, look at these figures for income tax for 1939 which was 16% and 1946 which was 57%. Can you understand why they jumped so fast? Why must we pay taxes like that for capitalists?

Capitalism is no good. We want a government like the Soviet Union and China, don't we, fellows?

At present, we must all learn and learn well. And, as soon as we have got home, we must clean out the capitalists and make up our own People's Government. We must do our part for its realization so that we won't be deceived again by men like Truman and MacArthur.

In January and February, 1951, this soldier wrote letters home stating that his Communist captors were treating him nicely and that he was being well-fed. But he died later that same year, apparently from malnutrition.

"The moral is clear," said Perry. "Once a man was stamped a reactionary, the Communists tended to shy away from him. Once he yielded, he was never thereafter his own master."

The Army believes from its study that a reactionary is right in keeping silent. There is a solid psychological reason for silence; and keeping silent benefits the prisoner, Major Segal told me. "Let's look at talking from the Communist side of the fence," he said. "We know from the returnees' accounts that once a man refused to talk, he was let alone. The Communist attitude seemed to be, 'The hell with him; he's not worth the trouble.' But those who yielded were forced to yield more and more. The Communists never stopped pumping them, because their own system never stops pumping them. It demands and demands, and enlarges and re-enlarges its demands, as if to prove to itself every day that its followers are still being faithful and haven't deviated an inch from the accepted line on which they were examined the day before. The system itself is paranoid. It's so suspicious that it demands daily checks and rechecks on what was said a month, a week, even an hour ago. That is why deviation is such a terrible crime behind the Iron Curtain—why elections must always be ninety-nine-and-two-thirds per cent in favor of the Party, with the fraction of opposition being thrown in as a sop to public credence. Why Yugoslavia is such a bugaboo. Communists are repressed and frightened people. The captor in Korea was in exactly the same position as the captive, except that he was farther along on the assembly line. He had his responsibilities to the system, and he was terrified if his fulfillment of them was called into question.

136

"A ridiculous but very revealing incident that took place in one of the prison camps illustrates this. After an indoctrination session, a GI was walking between his political instructor, who was expounding his view of some Marxist point, and the instructor's assistant. When the instructor finished, the prisoner said, pointing at the assistant, 'But Comrade Lee told me different.' For a moment, the two Communists stared at each other in amazement. Then both started running as fast as they could toward headquarters, each presumably to prevent the other's getting there first and denouncing him as a deviationist. Such conduct is understandable only when you realize that the basic psychological aim of Communism, which is at once its great strength and its great weakness, is the complete and utter isolation of the individual from his fellows—a really diabolical strategy.

"One of the big problems the Communists faced in the beginning, when they were organizing their government, was, of course, how to keep the minds of their people from straying away from strict loyalty to the party line. It was a police problem, but it would have required one policeman per person to watch every citizen constantly and see that no one developed deviationist tendencies. Then who would police the policeman? The problem seemed insoluble. So what did the Communists do? They simply evolved a means of isolating every person emotionally from every other person, permitting each one to turn only to the system for guidance and friendship. This was, in its way, a brilliant maneuver. It solved the problem without the use

137

of a single policeman, by creating another kind of police force, a completely effective one that operates around the clock without a hitch and requires no salaries. Some of the seemingly absurd and illogical demands the Communists made on the men in the camps in Korea make sense only when related to this psychological objective. The GI's, for instance, were puzzled when their captors bawled them out violently for some trivial offense such as not brushing their teeth. Of course, they rose meekly before everybody and publicly confessed they hadn't brushed their teeth. It seemed too foolish a thing to take a stand on. But once they had humbled themselves, even about something as minor as this, the Communists found it easier to get them to criticize themselves and other prisoners on more important questions. The men did not realize that acceding in these matters was alienating them subtly from each other and making them emotionally dependent on the system, till it was finally the only source of either praise or blame. Silence in the prison camps was the one sound antidote."

XII

Physical Aspects of Imprisonment

Food and Housing in Communist Camps—Chronology of Prisoner Acquisition—Prisoner Health and Chinese Medical Care

Food and housing in the Communist prisoner-of-war camps were bad, but not unbearable. They were at their worst at the start of the war and gradually improved. Unfortunately for the United States, the majority of our prisoners were with the Communists for most of the war. Colonel Perry went over this matter with me, showing me how the Communists had acquired their captives in the Korean conflict.

The war, Perry reminded me, had started on June 25, 1950, and could be divided into three distinct phases. The first was the initial Communist aggression, a strong push to the south that in a few short months in the summer of 1950 had all but wiped the peninsula clean of defenders.

139

The second phase was the almost successful counterattack by the defenders, which by late fall of 1950 had very nearly cleared the peninsula of aggressors. Then, in November of 1950, the Chinese Communists entered the war; they sent masses of troops into the line and forced the UN defenders to retreat southward. The retreat was halted near the middle of the peninsula about the beginning of 1951, and the third and longest phase of the war was waged there, in the vicinity of the former demarcation line between North and South Korea—an inconclusive series of actions that lasted for more than two-and-a-half years.

During the first phase and through most of the second, the North Koreans were the Communist enemy. By the time the Chinese came in, however, the North Korean Army had been virtually destroyed, and thereafter the Chinese ran the opposing side of the war. They were the masters of the situation and the bosses of the remaining North Koreans. There is little doubt, however, that the real enemy was the international Communist movement headed by Russia, in which both North Korea and China were relatively junior partners.

Most of the Army prisoners captured by the North Koreans and Chinese were taken early in the war, Colonel Perry told me. Of the 5,981 known to have been in enemy prison camps, 3,759, or almost two-thirds, were captured in the first six months of the war, during the first two mobile phases. Of the 2,222 others, 1,737 were captured in the first six months of 1951, so that only 485, or about 8 per cent were taken in the remaining two years of conflict. Thus the vast majority of our prisoners were in Communist hands for more than two-thirds of the war. The 44 per cent death rate among Army prisoners, which was somewhat higher than the over-all American figure, was also highest early in the war. A total of 2,634 Army prisoners died in captivity, of whom practically all—99.6 per cent—died in the first year; only nineteen men died in the following years.

After November, 1950, when the Chinese entered the war and took over the handling of prisoners, the prisoners' physical situation grew better, and the grievous conditions of diet and environment under the North Koreans gradually improved. In January, 1951, the Chinese started moving prisoners into the first of eight permanent camps well back of the fighting front, along a seventy-five mile stretch of the Yalu River, the northernmost boundary of North Korea.

My information on food and housing conditions in the Communist prisoner-of-war camps came from Major Clarence L. Anderson, a tall, dark-haired doctor in the Army Medical Corps. Major Anderson was on temporary duty in the Pentagon when I talked with him, and at present is attached to Letterman Army Hospital at San Francisco. Anderson was captured by the Chinese on November 3, 1950, at Unsan, North Korea. He was awarded the Distinguished Service Cross for his heroism in rounding up the wounded there and administering first aid to them, and for his refusal to leave them when the unwounded members of his battalion pulled out in retreat. In the weeks that followed his capture, he marched along Korean roads with columns of other prisoners, and was impounded in temporary holding camps. In January, 1951, Anderson was among the captives assigned to the first permanent camp established by the Chinese, in an evacuated portion of the Yalu River town of Pyoktong. This camp, later called Camp No. 5, was notorious among prisoners as the place where the most intensive Communist efforts were made to indoctrinate our men; it was also the headquarters for the entire prison-camp system in North Korea. During the first months of his almost three years of captivity, Anderson was allowed by the Communists to move freely among the camp compounds, giving medical attention to prisoners. His knowledge of conditions among prisoners was, therefore, much wider than that of the average captive. Most of them saw only the men in their own squads, but he saw men by the hundreds.

One of the most revealing things that Anderson noted as he and another American prisoner doctor made their rounds through the compound was the prisoners' attitude. Unfortunately, this was not "What can I do to help myself?" but "What can be done to help me?" He saw this attitude in practically every hut he visited. The net result was a kind of apathy, an inability to improvise or try new ways of life, which increased the prisoners' hardships. The attitude, for example, complicated the food situation, which was often critical in the early days.

Anderson told me that the Army combat ration is 3500

calories. By his estimate the prisoners' diet at its worst, early in the war, consisted of twelve hundred calories. This is inadequate, but a man will not starve on this intake. The food the North Koreans gave the prisoners was mainly cracked corn and millet, a cereal grass, unfamiliar to most Americans, the small seeds of which are eaten. Both corn and millet were prepared in the usual Korean manner by boiling in an iron pot hung over a fire. Many prisoners said they would not, or could not, eat this food. They seemed to be waiting, wistfully and unrealistically, for the arrival of American chow. The diet provided by the enemy was deficient in proteins, minerals, and vitamins. Sometimes these deficiencies were aggravated by the prisoners themselves. "For example," said Anderson, "during the worst early days the North Koreans gave us a few soybeans, which contained more protein than anything else we had. But the men disliked them. They believed, misguidedly, that they caused diarrhea. This was only because the beans had been insufficiently cooked, as some of the more intelligent men tried to make plain, but without success. After the Chinese took over, the prisoners complained so much about the beans that the enemy took them away. This left a big gap in our nutriment."

Anderson said that in his opinion most of the deaths from malnutrition among the prisoners were caused by lack of proteins, minerals, or vitamins, rather than by caloric deficiency, and that almost all cases of malnutrition were worsened to the point of seriousness, if not actually caused, by the prisoners' inability or disinclination to eat unfamiliar foods. Not long after the system of permanent camps was put into operation by the Chinese, the food improved, both in quality and quantity; and eventually the prisoners were fed a subsistence level of 2400 calories or more, which was pretty much maintained till the end of the war.

I asked Anderson about housing conditions in the camps, and about clothing. He said that since most of the camps were native villages from which the population had been evacuated, the prisoners were housed in the thatched huts that had belonged to the villagers. These had mud walls and were usually divided into two or three rooms. Some of the windows did, and some did not, have glass or panes made out of paper. The rooms were small, and prisoners slept on the floor. When the hut was crowded, the men sometimes had to accommodate themselves to a space per man half as wide as an upper berth in a pullman. A single electric-light bulb in the largest room was usually all the illumination. Heat came from a stove in the cellar that sent hot air through flues beneath the floor—a simple version of the radiant heat now fashionable with our architects, though in Korea it had the disadvantage of overheating the room periodically and making the floor too hot to lie on.

In winter, the weather in the camps was cold, the temperature falling to as low as 30 or 40 degrees below zero. At Camp No. 5, where Anderson was, the huts were in a valley, so that in winter they got only three hours of sunshine a day, and on any snow that did melt in this brief sun, a frozen crust soon formed. Summer weather was pleasant, somewhat like that in our Adirondacks, and prisoners were then allowed to swim in the Yalu. Clothing, on the whole, was adequate, and there was probably less suffering from lack of it than from any other cause. There was an issue of clothing two or three times a year, and generally the total issue for the year consisted of three outer shirts, three pairs of shorts, three pairs of socks, one quilted winter uniform, and two summer uniforms. The material was cotton and the color blue. Other winter clothes, issued somewhat irregularly, were quilted overcoats, fur-lined leather-and-canvas boots, and hair-lined caps. Summer uniforms were often worn in cold weather under the quilted clothing for greater warmth. Socks wore out first, and until new ones were issued, the prisoners improvised foot wrappings from various kinds of cloth.

From a medical standpoint, the prisoners withstood captivity fairly well, considering the harsh conditions imposed by their captors and by themselves. Pneumonia, dysentery, and malnutrition accounted for most of the deaths, Anderson said, and fatalities from all three could have been much reduced had there been adequate discipline operating within the units. He saw only one psychotic case in his camp and that man's period of unbalance was brief. For two or three weeks, he was out of contact with reality, and then he got better.

Health-promoting makeshifts of all kinds were used by the doctors in the camp in an effort to check physical deterioration among the prisoners. During the first winter, when the diet lacked all green vegetables and was at its worst, many of the men suffered what they called "bone pain"—shooting pangs which occurred during the night, mainly in the thighs. Anderson believed that it was pure and simple scurvy. The doctors eradicated it almost entirely with the coming of spring by advising the prisoners to boil and eat the young weeds that had sprung up around the various compounds. Surgical problems were handled with whatever primitive means was at hand. Since it was usually necessary to wait several weeks for a scalpel and the barest minimum of anesthetic materials from the Communists, the incision and drainage of such relatively common complaints as abscesses were performed without local anesthetics and with improvised instruments. A knife constructed from the arch of a combat boot and whetted on a stone might have to serve.

During the summer and fall of 1951, the few American and British doctors operating in the camp were gradually replaced by Chinese ones. "Most of these exhibited a wide range of professional incompetence," Anderson said. "The fact that under their treatment our prisoners fared no worse than they did is a marked tribute to the natural hardiness of the human body. The doctor put in the most responsible position was invariably the best orientated politically, not the best trained medically. Medicine was prescribed to relieve the symptoms, not to cure the basic condition; and it was a general rule that only one symptom would be treated at a time. Thus if a patient suffered from night blindness and diarrhea, he had to decide which of these complaints was bothering him more before he went on sick call, for he knew that he would not be treated for both conditions. The enemy also introduced us to several highly unusual types of medical treatment. One Chinese doctor used a series of short needles attached to spring vibrators for the elimination of pain. The needles were placed in the skin around the painful area, and then set to vibrating. Another doctor decided that all of our visual disturbances were caused by glaucoma, so he injected strong sodium chloride solution directly onto the eyeball. A favorite remedy for vitamin deficiency was a cupful of bile obtained from the gall bladders of slaughtered pigs. The enemy boasted of many cures with this regime, and in a sense he was right, because after one treatment our men became extremely wary about going on sick call a second time."

The most peculiar medical process of all was the tissue transplant, Anderson told me. This was a widely acclaimed Russian panacea. It had been touted by a Soviet publication a few years before as a cure not only for all diseases, including cancer, but also as a promoter of long life for those who underwent it. In the summer of 1951 it was tried on 56 prisoners seriously ill of various ailments. "An incision was made in the side of each patient, a small piece of chicken liver that had been soaked in penicillin solution was inserted, and the cut sewed up," Anderson said. "In 54 of the cases, the foreign matter sloughed out between the stitches; in the other two, it became a hard tender nodule. None of the men died and thus, the Chinese said, we were allowed to witness another miracle of Soviet medical science. Since the patients, simultaneously with the operation, were put on an attractive, high-calorie, high-protein, high-vitamin diet, there would seem to be some valid reason to doubt the enemy's claim of a professional miracle."

One of the worst problems in the camps, Anderson told me, was an illness known, at least in Camp No. 5, as "give-up-itis." Men afflicted with it seemed to will themselves to die. "You could follow the progress of the illness all too easily," Anderson said. "The sufferer first became despondent; then he lay down or covered his head with a blanket; then he wanted ice water to drink with his food; next no food, only water; and eventually, if he was not got to and helped, death would come. You could actually predict how long it would take such a man to die. If you didn't get to him within three weeks, he would be gone. However, if you caught him before that time, he could usually be saved. But in a camp of three thousand men, as Number Five was at the start, where there were only a few doctors and the movements of those restricted, it was hard to locate all these cases." I asked Anderson whether it was generally the younger or the older men who succumbed to "give-up-itis," and he said as a rule it was the younger. The treatment, once a case was discovered, was to force-feed the man, drag him upright, and compel him to move his limbs. Sometimes a man was choked till he consented to take food. If he spit out the food, it was scooped up and put back in his mouth. If, after a little of this, he agreed to eat something and sit up by himself, the doctor took his hands off him. But thereafter he was carefully watched. Provided the man did as he promised, in ten days he was usually all right. "One of the best ways to get a man on his feet initially," Anderson said, "was to make him so mad by goading, prodding, or blows that he tried to get up and beat you. If you could manage this, the man invariably got well."

Anderson said, he had one final thought about his experience, which concerned religion. "Or, anyhow, it has a spiritual side, I guess," he said. "In the first five months of captivity, we lost 1,500 Americans. Certainly, it was lack of discipline. Good discipline would have prevented most of it, I grant you. But so would social responsibility, the feeling for your fellowman that runs so importantly through all religions, the 'Do unto others as you would have them do unto you' theme. I know I would like to see my kids, every kid in America, taught and retaught the importance of the Golden Rule to help them better endure—if they have to face it—the kind of situation we had to endure."

The Army study had not been able to find that a stated religious preference, or a lack of it, was a factor in producing either collaborators or reactionaries, I reminded Anderson. This was not what he meant, Anderson said. Announced adherence on a personnel card to some denomination or other was definitely not what he had in mind.

What he was referring to, he stressed, was the kind of religion that touches a man inside and causes him to act, however dark the situation, as an ethical, fearless human being.

XIII

Ethical and Moral Problems

Army Awards to Valorous Prisoners—Lieutenant Colonel John J. Dunn and Chaplain Emil J. Kapaun—Lack of Group Discipline Among Prisoners

In its study of the conduct of its prisoners of war the Army was just as careful to look for good behavior as for bad, I was told by Colonel Trammell. The Adjutant General's office, assisted by the same two groups in G-2 that hunted for evidence of collaboration in our prisoners, used the same standards in searching the files of the returnees for outstanding examples of patriotic behavior. For the Army felt, Trammell explained, that commending the good soldier was in every way as important as censuring the bad one. As a result of the Army's work in this field, 138 men were considered for some mark of honor for valorous or meritorious conduct while a prisoner of war. Of this number, 55 individuals or their survivors were presented with awards: two Legions of Merit, eighteen Bronze Stars, and thirty-five Army Commendation Ribbons with Metal Pendant. The publicity on these awards was almost nil compared with that which attended the prisoner-of-war trials.

Equally overshadowed by the prisoner trials were the exploits of some of these prison-camp resisters. This was unfortunate. Because of the notoriety which accompanied the trials, the impression was perhaps unavoidable that all Army captives in Korea were weaklings, collaborators, or both. This was far from true, Trammell told me. He paraphrased for me some official documents relating to two of the men decorated, Lieutenant Colonel John J. Dunn, and Captain Emil J. Kapaun, a chaplain, whose parents were presented with his award posthumously.

Dunn, according to the records, consistently overextended himself on rearward marches to holding centers in the early days of the war by helping carry the ill and dying. Later he constantly fought for an improvement of living conditions in the compounds, and on numerous occasions he risked punishment to intercede forcefully and effectively with enemy authorities for comrades in trouble and to safeguard important military information that was current among the group of reactionaries he led. His brave and intelligent leadership and guidance saved the lives of many prisoners who otherwise would have died.

Kapaun, a Catholic chaplain, an outstanding member of an outstanding corps, had elected to be captured rather than retreat in order to stay with his regiment's wounded. He successfully fought indoctrination among the men, ministered to the sick and dying of all faiths, and, like the good foot-soldier he was, stole food from the enemy during the blackest days of internment to supplement the insufficient diet and to support the weak. Selfish thieves who hoarded their gains were shamed into contributing them to the common fund when Father Kapaun, walking into a hut, laid his on the floor, and, bowing his head, quietly asked all present to join in a prayer of thanks to God for providing what could be equally shared. He died in a prison hospital of malnutrition. He literally killed himself, the records show, by his unstinting devotion to others, laying down his life for the principle of self-sacrifice as humbly as, for its sake also, he had originally allowed himself to be captured.

Group behavior is a strange phenomenon. It is dominated, unquestionably, by the strongest influence in the group. Kapaun was his group's strongest force. And he was a force for good. Love of man, love of country, love of God were higher among the prisoners around him while he lived. In the drear days of early captivity, he affected for the better, and made a better American of, every man he came in contact with. None of them will ever forget him. His individual influence, even if slender, extends effectively across the world to wherever the men now live who knew him. Kapaun's was one of the more glorious mortalities in the sad statistic of 38 percent prisoner deaths.

Apropos of the high prisoner death rate, I gathered that the Army felt its losses were due not so much to the Communists' disregard of the provisions of the Geneva Convention—although this was unquestionably contributory—as to a breakdown of discipline among the prisoners themselves. Many men after capture appeared to have lost all sense of allegiance, not only to their country but to their fellow-prisoners. Psychologists explain these lapses of conduct by the fact that all prisoners are initially in a state of shock because of the position in which they find themselves; furthermore, our men were peculiarly susceptible to this disorganization because they had come into battle straight from soft, peacetime lives.

"While this may be an explanation, it is not an excuse, and the Army does not consider it as such," a spokesman had told me earlier. "The Army has to face the facts it has discovered, and the Army has to correct them."

I asked Major Anderson whether what he had seen during his prison-camp experience had been in line with these findings. In general, he told me, he had to corroborate what I had heard. "It is a sad fact, but it is a fact, that the men who were captured in large groups early in the war too often became unmanageable," Anderson said. "They refused to obey orders, and they cursed and sometimes struck officers trying to enforce orders. The result was a general collapse of that unity that is so essential to survival in enemy hands. The chaos, of course, was encouraged by the Communists, who told the captives immediately after they were taken that rank no longer existed among them, that they were all equal as simple prisoners of war released from capitalist bondage. At first, the badly wounded suffered most. On marches back from the line, where prisoners were collected, to temporary holding camps, casualties on litters were often callously abandoned beside the road. The able-bodied refused to carry them even when their officers commanded them to do so. If a Communist guard ordered a litter shouldered, our men obeyed; otherwise the wounded were left alone to die. On the march, in the temporary camps, and in the permanent ones, the strong regularly took food from the weak. There was no discipline to prevent it. Many men were sick, and instead of being helped and nursed by the well, the sick men were ignored or, worse, even helped to their deaths. Dysentery, a debilitating disease, was common. Sufferers from it often became too weak to walk. On winter nights, helpless men whose clothes stank from their excreta were rolled outside the huts by their comrades and left to die in the cold."

A prisoner could not challenge another to act like a soldier because too often the other man felt himself no longer to be a soldier—and said so. As Anderson and his fellow doctor made their daily rounds in the permanent camp, the only means by which they could arouse a sense of responsibility in the men was by enjoining them to act not like soldiers—because this had been tried and had failed—but like human beings: to wash once in a while, to keep their clothes and quarters moderately clean, and to lend each other an occasional helping hand. This very weak plea, which was not always successful, was the only one to which there was any response at all, Anderson said.

When I asked Anderson the thing that struck him most

155

forcibly about the way the men reacted to prison-camp conditions, he said, "It was their almost universal inability to adjust to a primitive situation—a regrettable lack of the old Yankee ingenuity, you might say. This reaction was partially—but only partially, I believe—the result of the psychic shock of being captured. It was also, I think, the result of some new failure in the childhood and adolescent training of our young men—a new softness." Many men withdrew into a life of inactivity. Very few seemed interested even in providing themselves with the basic necessities of food, warmth, and shelter. For example, the Chinese gave them a chance to go up into the nearby hills and bring down firewood, but the prisoners were too inert to do it. The whole physical routine of Army life seemed to collapse in the prison camps.

Again the trouble seems to have been a lack of discipline. Although the Communists had segregated the officers, Anderson said, each compound still had a senior noncommissioned officer, who, if he had exercised control through the chain of command, could have improved the lot of the entire group. "Let me show you what I mean by a healthy prisoner organization. If things had been done right, the men in a squad or a platoon would have got up at a specified time in the morning at an order from their senior member, washed, and lined up for chow. They would have eaten indoors or out, depending on the temperature, and then cleaned up the area, gathered wood, and got water. Each man would have seen to keeping his body and his clothing free of lice by squeezing the insects between two fingernails, an important and time-consuming task in a situation where the productive consumption of time is psychologically important. Each group, of course, had men who were sick and must be cared for. If a unit had been run properly, men would have been detailed to look after the sick—wash their clothes, give them water, prevent them from lying in one position too long and getting bedsores, and scrounge better food for them. In the Korean prison camps, thigh muscles, apparently because of poor diet, often contracted so the knee was bent; sometimes a man could not rise after a night's sleep. A little massage would correct this, and it could have been done by the other men in the hut; if it was not done, the man became a casualty, unnecessarily. In camp, anything that gets prisoners' minds off themselves is good for them, so the leader of a well-run outfit would have organized calisthenics and games, and got the men to make chess and checker sets. If this sort of disciplined program had been carried out by each unit in the camps, our men would have maintained their identities as loyal American soldiers and would have functioned practically as such. Captivity is a miserable situation under the best of conditions. But with proper organization it would have been much easier for our men than it was. The nightmare of guilt that still haunts so many of those who returned would have been avoided, and, most important, more of us would have returned."

XIV

Turkish Triumph— American Defeat

Behavior of Other Than Army Prisoners in Korea—The Air Force—The Marines—The Turks—Instances of Successful Mass Resistance by Army Prisoners

So far we have discussed only the behavior of United States Army prisoners of war in Korea. How did other prisoners of the Chinese Communists act? Were the techniques to which they were subjected the same? Is it possible to show, in the light of what they went through, whether they had better, comparable, or worse records? And more important, do their experiences tend to confirm or refute the conclusions the Army has drawn from the experiences of its own men?

In a sense, the other prisoners can be thought of as control groups. Should it be found that their previous training was different from the Army's and that, also, their

158

behavior as prisoners of war was different, there is a strong presumption that a connection exists between their training and their prison-camp behavior. Should it be found that this training-behavior pattern is present in more than one of the groups, the presumption becomes very strong, indeed.

Americans not in the Army repatriated from Korea consisted of 235 Air Force, 196 Marine, and 31 Navy personnel. The Army study did not investigate their actions, but their own services did and published data on what they found.

Also returned during *Operation Big Switch* were roughly 1400 prisoners from the troops of other nations contributing to the U.N. police force in Korea—the majority of them British. There were slightly less than a thousand from the United Kingdom, and a mixed group of about sixty Canadians, Australians, and South Africans. These men were handled and evaluated by British groups. The remainder of the prisoners, 308 in all, were processed by the Army as the service in charge of the over-all prisoner repatriation program. In this group were 229 Turks, 40 Filipinos, 22 Colombians, 12 French, 2 Greeks, 2 Netherlanders, and 1 Belgian.

The largest non-Army contingent of Americans was from the Air Force. This unit differed markedly from the Army, both in its own composition and in its treatment by the enemy. More than two-thirds of its members were officers, compared with 5 per cent for the Army. Over half had some college training as against 5 per cent again for the Army. Not only was its social and educational level higher—so was its value to enemy intelligence officers. An airman is highly technically trained. He carries in his head routine information about aerial equipment and combat tactics of much greater value to the enemy than any information possessed by the average GI. In addition, his combat conditions, which involve sedentary activity in rather cramped quarters, tend perhaps to make him physically a little less hardy than a hill-climbing infantryman.

The Communists treated the relatively small number of Air Force men very differently from the way they treated the large masses of Army prisoners. Virtually no indoctrination was tried. An Air Force prisoner was given individual treatment which much more nearly approximated that accorded a political prisoner in Russia from whom a false confession is wanted. The ideal end result of this kind of treatment is at least a temporary alteration of character. Isolation and extreme psychological pressures were the techniques used. A prisoner was kept by himself, often in the most confined and uncomfortable surroundings. His sleep and his food were limited. His wounds or ailments, if any, were often left untended. As fatigue set in, he was worked upon almost ceaselessly by an interrogator, or a series of interrogators, who drummed home hour after hour, day after day, the thought that he was helpless, that he was alone, that his comrades and his country had forgotten him, and that his only hope for life was to cooperate. On top of this (as sometimes does and sometimes does not occur in this type of handling of political prisoners), the Air Force reported numerous cases of beatings and gross physical brutality. This sort of treatment, which is standard police practice in the Communist states of Eastern Europe, is successful in getting confessions in better than 90 per cent of the cases in which it is tried; and the usual time of success is twelve weeks, according to men in this country who have studied the matter.

The chief aim of the Communists with regard to Air Force prisoners was to extract from them false confessions of bacteriological warfare. In February, 1952, the Chinese started their campaign, using fifty-nine Air Force men, thirty-eight of whom eventually made some kind of confession. Twenty-three of these confessions were used for enemy propaganda purposes. Fifteen per cent of those men who yielded did so after one month or less of pressure. A larger percentage, obviously, despite everything the Chinese could do, refused to confess after twenty-four weeks of intensive treatment, a notable achievement when placed beside the Eastern European figures for compliance and time of compliance. In this adamant group was a first lieutenant who, in the words of an Air Force research official, ". . . after being classified as a war criminal was interrogated and pressured for four months by the Chinese Communists. Eight times he was ordered to confess, offered relief if he did, death if he didn't. Eight times he refused. He was stood at attention for five hours at a time, was confined eight days in a doorless cell less than six feet long, held to the ground by two guards while a third kicked and slapped him, stood at attention another time for twenty-two hours until he fell and was then hit while lying down with the side of a hatchet and stood up for two hours. He was interrogated three hours with a spotlight six inches from his face. He was ordered to confess while a pistol was held at the back of his head. He was placed under a roof drain all night during a rainstorm. He was left without food for three days. He was put before a firing squad and given a last chance, hung by hands and feet from the rafters of a house. When he still refused, the Chinese Communists let him alone. They had apparently given him up as an impossible case. He came back alive."

The statement made by another Air Force resister, Captain Theodore Harris, has received wide circulation and respect not only in his own but in other services. His story has been often told since his return. Harris, held by the Communists in solitary confinement for fourteen months, much of it spent handcuffed in a small thatched hole in the ground, was one of the more intractable captives of the war. His prison philosophy, he told those who met him upon his release at Panmunjom, was "If I can't go back with my self-respect, I won't go back at all."

It is difficult to compare Army and Air Force prisoner actions because of the difference in treatment. A comparison is possible, however, between Army prisoners and Marine Corps prisoners. The Marines had both air and infantry prisoners taken by the enemy. Thirty-one Marine fliers were handled like Air Force prisoners, and the rest of the

Marine Corps prisoners, who were ground troops, received the Army treatment. The Marine Corps feels it had a substantially better prisoner record both before and after entering camp.

To begin with, a much smaller percentage of Marines were taken prisoner. The total strengths of the Marine Corps and the Army operating in Korea during the war were, respectively, 129,500 and approximately 900,000 men. The Marines had 227 men taken prisoner, or 1 in 570, as contrasted with the Army's 1 in 150 men. Once in camp, the Marines feel, their edge continued. Thirty-one Marines died in imprisonment. This amounts to 13 per cent. The Army figure was something better than three times that. Finally, the Marine Corps states, its men offered sturdier resistance to indoctrination.

In prison camp Marine officers and men were segregated and subjected to the same interrogation and indoctrination as were the Army personnel. After repatriation, 52 Marines were investigated by the Corps; 49 were cleared of any wrongdoing in a preliminary examination of their behavior. Two others, both fliers, were subsequently cleared of misconduct by a court of inquiry and reinstated, subject to restricted assignments. A third was dismissed from the service by a board of inquiry for fraternizing with the enemy. This man was the Corps' sole disciplinary casualty of the Korean prison camps.

Fourteen Marines admitted signing peace appeals or petitions of some sort. But the Commandant, after suitable inquiry, decided they had done nothing dishonorable. No other Marines signed any appeals or petitions. No Marines participated in any Communist-sponsored oratorical contest, or in any Communist-sponsored play, or wrote for the Communist publication, *Toward Truth and Peace*, or took part in any activity connected with the propaganda agency, the Central Peace Committee. The prisoner of war experience in Korea constituted no real problem to its service, the Marines feel.

The Marine Corps believes the reason its men resisted indoctrination lies in their leadership, discipline, and rigorous training. A spokesman commenting on this not long ago said, "The military organization with a Marine is never excused. It exists wherever Marines might be—at a swimming pool in the States, in a movie, on a train, certainly in a battle, and certainly in a prison camp. Marines willingly accept the military organization, the leadership that motivates it, and the discipline that makes it work. I think the performance of our Korean prisoners of war demonstrates that."

Among the non-American prisoners, the Turks were the largest group the Army had data on. Theirs was an outstanding record both as regards death rate and conduct in captivity. After their release the 229 Turkish prisoners were questioned extensively about their prison experiences by members of the Army Joint Intelligence Processing Team that was stationed in Tokyo. From these interrogations and from eyewitness reports by our own men, the Army obtained its information.

Out of the entire number of Turks that fell into enemy hands, not a single one died in captivity. This is especially surprising in view of the fact that almost half these men were wounded when they were captured. "It is a remarkable record," Colonel Perry told me. "All the more so by comparison with our own. At Death Valley, one of the temporary prison camps established by the Communists in the early days of the war, into which the sick and wounded poured for weeks in a steady stream, the Turks lost not a single man out of a hundred and ten interned. American losses during this same period at this same camp were, we estimate, from four hundred to eight hundred dead out of fifteen hundred to eighteen hundred prisoners interned."

The secret of the Turks' astonishing record, Perry said, was the strict discipline they maintained from the time of their capture till their release. "Of course, some of them got sick in camp," he said, "as did prisoners of other nationalities. But when a Turk got sick, the rest nursed him back to health. If a sick Turk was ordered to the hospital, two well Turks went along. They ministered to him hand and foot while he was there, and when he was discharged, brought him back to the compound in their arms. They shared their clothing and their food equally. When the Communists did the cooking for the camp, two Turks were dispatched to bring back food for the group, and it was divided in equal portions down to the last morsel. There was no hogging, no rule of dog eat dog."

I asked Colonel Perry how the Turks had reacted toward indoctrination, and he replied that they had withstood it almost one hundred per cent. Because their chain of command remained unbroken, they were able to present a completely united front to pressure, despite the fact that their officers and men were segregated like the rest of the prisoners. To illustrate this, the Colonel read to me from the account of a Turkish officer's prison experience, given to one of our interrogators. "I told the Chinese commander of the camp that while we were a unit, I was in charge of my group," the Turkish officer said. "If he wanted anything done, he was to come to me, and I would see that it was done. When he removed me, the responsibility would fall not on him, but on the man next below me, and after that on the man below him. And so on, down through the ranks, until there were only two privates left. Then the senior private would be in charge. They could kill us, I told him, but they couldn't make us do what we didn't want to do. Discipline was our salvation, and we all knew it. If a Turk had responded to an order from his superiors to share his food or lift a litter the way I understand some of your men did, he would literally have had his teeth knocked in. Not by his superior, either, but by the Turk nearest to him."

When the prisoners were first segregated according to rank and nationality, the Turks were singled out as a special target of indoctrination. In the beginning, the Chinese attempted to indoctrinate them by presenting mild lectures through an interpreter. Two Chinese tried this without success. The Turks claimed they did not understand what the Chinese were talking about, and heckled the speakers by asking ridiculous questions, some in English, some in their native tongue. After this experience, the Chinese imported a longtime Turkish resident of Russia, who lived with the Turks. Through him they attempted to promote some kind of discussion group within their ranks. The Turks chose to take the man as a joke. They made life very unpleasant for him, and before long he took an unannounced departure both from his assignment and the camp area. Then Monica Felton, the English Communist, visited the Turks, and said she was bringing them greetings from their neighbors, the Russians. She spent several days with them, trying to soften them up intellectually. They rejected her efforts and presented her with an insulting document whose burden was to peddle her Communist doctrine elsewhere. Next the Chinese brought in a Caucasian who had lived in the Middle East and spoke Turkish. He, too, failed to get indoctrination going. Finally James Veneris, one of the United States nonrepatriates, who spoke both Greek and Turkish, was appointed by the Chinese as the group's indoctrinator. Veneris eventually quit in disgust, although he was severely criticized by the Chinese for doing so.

The Turks' group spirit is illustrated by the following incident. Two Turkish prisoners helped in the preparation of a self-critical petition in which certain uncomplimentary remarks were directed at their government. The Army considered this a relatively minor thing; but feeling against these two men by the other Turks ran high. They were completely ostracized for the rest of the period of imprisonment, and apparently came to fear for their lives. During the repatriation process they asked for and received from the Army protective custody to guard them from the wrath of their compatriots. These two men were the only Turks who could be called collaborators.

Apart from indoctrination, the Turks pretty well flouted the authority of their Chinese captors. They broke rules and often refused to obey ostensibly reasonable requests. They simply declined to cooperate, and eventually the Communists left them alone. It was generally believed that the Chinese feared the Turks to some degree because they stuck together as a group and resisted as a group. Their discipline and military organization saw them through as prisoners with no fatalities and virtually no indoctrination.

Additional evidence of the success of Communist techniques with our men was that many of the Army repatriates came home thinking of themselves not as a group bound by common ties and loyalties, but as isolated individuals. This attitude showed only too clearly in the way they answered questions about their service outfit during the repatriation process. When a Turk was asked what his outfit was, he would answer proudly, "Third Company, First Regiment, Turkish Volunteer Brigade," or whatever the proper designation might be. The GI's too often responded with the number of their prison camp and the company or platoon they had belonged to in it.

Despite the successes that we have had to recognize, the enemy program was by no means irresistible even against the average, run-of-the-mine Army prisoner. "That was the great lesson we learned from our studies," Colonel Perry told me. "The enemy's success depended absolutely on our men's compliance." Perhaps half a dozen times during the war, there were instances of organized mass resistance on the part of the prisoners. For example, on May Day, 1952, the Communists brought out red banners and new uniforms and told the prisoners they would march in a parade. Certain individuals passed the word not to fall out for the parade, "no matter what." The prisoners refused to fall out and the parade was not held. In this case, the suspected leaders were jailed, but there was no punishment for the rest. As another example, the following year the Chinese wanted to take pictures of a group of prisoners exercising, but the prisoners would not cooperate. One man walked off and the rest followed. The Chinese were furious, but took no retributive action. On another occasion when a prisoner was being unjustly treated, the man's company fell out en masse and demanded his release within half an hour on threat of mutiny. The prisoner was released by the Chinese and there was no retaliation. "In each case, the prisoners won," said Colonel Perry. "It had to be so. Because there is no way of compelling a group, through methods of mass psychological pressure, to do something it says firmly it won't do. Mass resistance in that case always wins."

XV

Why Our Discipline Failed

One Officer's Views on Discipline During Korean War—
Doolittle Report Recommendations Criticized—Ordinances
Mentioned for Culling Unmotivated Personnel—Selling Army
to Recruits on Basis of Honorable Service Rather Than Material
Gain

Since lack of discipline seemed to be one of the most critical
deficiencies that the Army had discovered in its study, I
sought to obtain some insight on this important matter.
The pros and cons of the subject were outlined for me in
detail by a combat officer who was a veteran of both the
Korean conflict and World War II. He had some interesting ideas on this and on related matters which he had de-
rived from work on the prisoner-of-war study, in which he
had taken an active part. I will call him Colonel Brown
because his remarks are perhaps too unconventional to be
given without a pseudonym for name and rank.

"Our discipline was frankly shot in the early days of the

war," Brown said. "One of the really shocking things about the first year or so in Korea was the scores of men held back of the lines in punitive stockades, charged with misbehavior before the enemy. None were executed, so far as I know, although in time of war this offense carries the death penalty. During this period sizable units under fire in more than one division just broke and ran away. Many times the enemy was mistakenly given credit for destroying a particular group, whereas actually, at the time of his attack, our group as a fighting group never existed. Men refused to help each other or hang together. Groups as large as four hundred surrendered in a body. My God, with that number you can give a pretty good account of yourself with sticks!

"The chaos was as evident in little details as in the big things. For example, water discipline, a primary necessity for soldiers in the summer, was shockingly remiss. Men swigged too heavily on the canteen although ordered not to do so—and in the heat they were soon knocked out. In the old Army they would have gone dry if commanded till their tongues hung out—but not in this one. Care of the feet, so critical to an infantryman, was often completely disregarded because none of the officers could, or would, enforce it. Dozens of hospital cases of frostbite, fungus, and infection resulted from disregard of this one simple elementary rule—an incidence out of all proportion to what had happened in other wars. As a result of these and other perfectly idiotic infractions, in the first four months of the war we had nearly twice as many nonbattle as battle casualties, an almost incredible record. No wonder the prisoners folded up like paper dolls before the indoctrinators.

"Loyalty to one's fellow soldiers and to one's country should be intrinsically inherent in every person, certainly in every American, you would say," Brown went on. "But to speak a widely-known truth, a certain number of those men who have come into the Army after the Second World War, and as far as that goes today, are completely without loyalty. This means it is necessary to impose a hard, almost blind, discipline to get real efficiency. Look at the juvenile delinquents, the confirmed adult-haters, the slum kids who know nothing but the dog-eat-dog rule. How can you deal with them without discipline? A juvenile delinquent may never become the ideal American soldier, because the chances are he will never be able to rise above blind discipline to the more preferable level of discipline with initiative. But with hard discipline he and others like him will make satisfactory soldiers. I've seen the Foreign Legion in bivouac and in action. Although perhaps its performance under all conditions may not square precisely with the West Point optimum, I can't erase from my memory how well the Legion's hard discipline welds together men of many countries—some of them the adult counterparts of juvenile delinquents—into an effective fighting unit. From the ethical point of view, I admit that discipline alone isn't the entirely satisfactory answer to Communist indoctrination of prisoners. Ideally there should be strong and sound motivation to be an American always, no matter what the circumstances. And this motivation should be as strong as that of the Communists, many of whom, my friend, are strongly motivated, indeed. But if firm discipline is imposed on top of sound motivation to be an American, two helpful things happen. Peak military efficiency is reached. And so is resistance to Communist indoctrination.

"The Army, in my opinion, should get back to basic principles, both in discipline and techniques," Brown continued. "The First World War had a marching army; the Second World War a riding army. For future safety, the two must be combined. Because a mechanized army has no provision for the failure of mechanization. If tires, gas, the footing fails—the mechanized army fails. When trucks fail, the truck-accustomed soldier fails. A riding soldier asked to walk is lost. In Korea sick prisoners lay down by the side of the road, thinking they would be picked up by a truck the way they are in our Army, which runs ambulances behind prisoner columns for stragglers. But this didn't happen. Men walked or died as prisoners in the Korean War. And presumably any future war with Communist enemies will be the same. The men on our side should know this.

"If we had had good discipline in Korea, do you suppose the following would have been the partial record of one physically powerful and criminally inclined prisoner on the march to his eventual prisoner camp? He stole the watch of a fellow captive and pushed the victim, when he objected, to his death over a cliff; he dumped a wounded comrade he was carrying from a litter into a stream, causing

173

him to drown, simply because he was tired of carrying him; and he struck a superior officer in the face with his fist when ordered by that officer to stop beating and robbing other sick and dying prisoners."

Brown believes that the Army's lack of discipline stemmed mainly from the acceptance by the service of the recommendations of the Doolittle Board. This board was set up in 1945 to iron out inequities that were alleged to have existed at that time between the officers and the enlisted man. The board was headed by the famous aviator who was then, before the creation of a separate Air Force, a member of the Army. "Theoretically, the Doolittle Board seemed like a good idea—at the time. Actually, the way it worked out, it just about destroyed Army morale," said Brown. "To arrive at its recommendations, it interviewed forty-two so-called representative witnesses, and studied the contents of approximately a thousand letters, many of them written by former service personnel who manifestly hated regimentation and resented the loss of their personal identity within the vast military machine that had to be manufactured to do the job in World War Two. Was this slender sampling a sufficiently broad base on which to make the far-reaching decisions that were handed down by the Board? It seems questionable particularly in the light of the fact that in 1945 the Army had a peak strength of over eight million men. However, in that year the war had been won, and everybody was thinking in terms of manning peacetime garrisons—and not of the Army's main purpose of fighting and winning conflicts, worldwide and otherwise.

174

"Without going into the precise history and exact recommendations of the board, I think it can be fairly stated that its suggestions greatly narrowed the distance between the commissioned and the noncommissioned ranks, all with the laudable purpose of making the enlisted man happier with his lot. What the board's theoreticians did not realize, however, was that there is no narrowing that gap without great loss of military efficiency. Consequently, the Doolittle Board had two bad effects on discipline. The first was at the level of the company-grade officer. This highly important administrative official felt that he had been stripped of his punitive power by the board's actions, particularly his power of summary court-martial. As a matter of fact, he had *not* been deprived of the power in every conceivable instance, but the important thing was that he *thought* that he had. Admittedly there were things to be said on the other side. Admittedly there have been abuses of the summary court-martial in the Army's history. Conditions like those shown in the film *From Here to Eternity* and in certain books and other motion pictures depicting Army life and mistreatment of inferiors by superiors have not been unknown. But there are two ways to limit such abuses. One is to take power away from your company officer. The other is to improve the quality of those same officers. The Doolittle Board, with its recommendation of the first course, certainly took the wrong approach in my opinion. Because of what the board did, junior officers refused to take responsibility, understandably feeling that they lacked the authority to enforce it. And as a result, discipline sagged. Commissioned ranks hesitated to give unpopular orders; and things got done, if they got done at all, more on a basis of friendship between officers and men than because of authority vested in the officers, a very loose and unworkable method.

"The second thing the Doolittle Board did was to undermine to a dangerous degree the influence of the noncommissioned officer, who is the backbone of the Army. Since the company-grade officers thought they lacked the punitive power to back up the decisions of the noncoms, these lesser officers, too, shied away from responsibility. As a result, far too frequently in the Army it has become an accepted notion that a private should take orders only from a commissioned officer. In the old Army an enlisted man looked up to a corporal or a sergeant as though he were almost God Almighty. And it was a good thing, too. Now, because of the Doolittle Board, stripers or nonstripers often feel they are simply enlisted men together, and as a result, affairs in a squad can get into as sorry a condition as they did in Korea.

"To cap the general sabotaging of discipline, the Doolittle Board emphasized—quite unintentionally and without malice, of course—a special tool by giving new prominence to the Inspector General system. This system has always existed in the Army, making it possible for any man to present wrongs for redress without going through ordinary command channels. But the Doolittle Board recommendations turned the spotlight on it. On the surface, this

176

emphasis would seem fine because the man's beef must be genuine, or, supposedly, the complainant gets into trouble with the Inspector General. But how does it work out in actuality? Let's say some resolute captain or sergeant determines to whip his unit into shape with the aid of a little old-fashioned discipline. For the sake of illustration, let's make the man a sergeant with a squad. He's working it over—and a private feels put upon. What happens? The private goes to the Inspector General's office and states that his particular sergeant uses bad language and threats. In fact, he has told the private profanely that if he doesn't get a particular portion of his anatomy out to the drillground pronto it will be swiftly booted there. The I.G.'s office must then by its rules—which the Doolittle Board underlined—investigate and call the sergeant before it. If he can satisfactorily explain his actions, the investigation is closed on a face-to-face basis and that's the end of it, generally speaking, as far as all sides are concerned. If it appears, however, that there is some basis for the charge of mistreatment, the I.G. may direct a formal inquiry and trial whose verdict may put a black mark on the sergeant's record.

"But even if this second step isn't taken, what is the *practical* effect of a policy that permits a soldier to appeal from his superior's authority to a third person who was not present when the authority in question was exercised? It is the complete gutting of discipline. Imagine what it would be like trying to control a child, if, before you could impose discipline, you had first to present the problem for the

177

minister's approval when he came to dinner on Sunday. What kind of children would a family have under those circumstances? If only some of the blessed parents who have made so much trouble for the Army by writing their congressmen and in general raising a ruckus about the brutal and outrageous discipline being imposed on their boys could know the real and vital necessity for this discipline, they might quit being a thorn in the Army's side. Just as obedience is necessary for the general good in the home, so it is in the Army—only there the stakes, which may be the survival of all the men in the unit, are much, much higher. Let us say, for the sake of example, that the I.G.'s office intrudes even once a week on a determined sergeant or a company commander. You can guess the kind of discipline you'll have in a couple of months in that squad or in that company. And that's the kind of discipline, generally speaking, that we've got in the Army today. And we've got that kind of discipline whether or not people are *actually* going to the I.G. As a noncom or a company commander, you've only got to *know* somebody this has happened to, or hear about it, from a pal, and your discipline starts to lack the firmness it should have.

"Now don't misunderstand me. The discipline I'm talking about has nothing to do with the you-dig-a-hole-and-then-you-fill-it-up-because-I-say-so sort of thing. To far too many Americans this attitude, and this attitude alone, means Army discipline. Naturally they resent it. But what I have in mind amounts almost to a creed—a family relationship, if you will—in which responsibility is shared by both sides. The good officer maintains authority and efficiency in his unit by creating an atmosphere of trust between himself and his men. He can be beloved for this, too. He can be beloved simply because he is able, like a good father, to give consistent direction. He doesn't vacillate. He isn't harsh. But neither is he overly permissive. Above all, he isn't permissive. What he says, in effect, is 'Here, soldier, for your lawful obedience, which I've exacted from you, I give you back your self-esteem. You are now a better soldier—heightened and more complete. Our unit is now a better unit—heightened and more complete. And this is so because you trust me and I trust you.' And psychologically this works out because as the efficient commander, within the framework of discipline, gives trust and responsibility to his men, he gets back, as surely as sunshine follows the rain, obedience and authority in return.

"But the Doolittle Board turned up the permissive road, giving us a loose, undisciplined system in the Army. Now what happens under this loose, undisciplined system in combat? A company commander calls his platoon leaders together to give attack orders. These have filtered to him down the chain of command from battalion headquarters, which got them from regiment, which got them from division headquarters. The platoon leaders, who are commissioned officers, go back to the platoon command posts and give the orders to the assembled squad leaders—noncommissioned officers over about ten men. In combat the squads may well be the largest tactical unit that will meet the enemy as a group. The next day they may be spread over scores of yards of the front under heavy fire. Attack or retreat plans have to be altered unexpectedly, and then there is no one to give the order but a noncommissioned officer. Acceptance of the order may mean the difference between life and death to the individual and to the group. The only way to get in the habit of obeying orders from a noncommissioned officer is to obey them at all times, implicitly, on the parade ground, in the barracks, on public streets, everywhere. This habit builds up the required confidence in the noncommissioned officer who, in combat after a day or two, or perhaps even after only a few hours, may end up commanding the platoon. The idea that enlisted men should take orders only from a commissioned officer is just plain nonsense. Hell, I've had the three squads in a platoon spread over forty miles during a rapid advance in a very fluid combat situation. Admittedly that's an unusual situation. But to have three squads pinned down by heavy fire in hilly terrain over a front of five hundred yards, each facing an entirely different set of circumstances, and a highly superior, an equal, and an inferior enemy force is *not* unusual. Under these circumstances, how could a commissioned officer give a sensible, on-the-spot, emergency order, sight unseen, to his enlisted men? Those men would have to depend on the good sense and experience of the noncommissioned officer over them—but the Doolittle Board brained the noncommissioned officer, and with him the real chain of command. And with that, I make so bold as to say, the real combat efficiency of the Army. I know I'm hipped on the subject of discipline. But I've seen it work. I know it works. And I've never seen any substitute for it.

"Other less important problems arise, too, under our present lax system of discipline. I've come up against the results many times in army stockades. What happens is this: a soldier commits a minor offense—a short period of unauthorized absence, or something like that—and instead of a simple, direct, clearly defined punitive measure being imposed on him at once by his immediate superior, he's called in by the company commander and talked to and explained at and, in a way, he's sort of asked not to do it again. So, of course, in many of the cases, it naturally happens once again, and yet again, and ultimately the company commander or the responsible officer finds that he can no longer avoid bringing this man to the attention of higher authorities; and he applies to the regimental commander to convene, not a summary, but a full-scale court-martial. At this court-martial the accused appears with a series of notations on his record stating that he has repeatedly been AWOL for short periods, repeatedly been uncooperative with his superiors, repeatedly been such-and-such and so on, and consequently he is sentenced to six months imprisonment, or to a punitive discharge, or both. And so it happens that a number of GI's who are not exactly broad thinkers or deep philosophers in any sense of the word have sat across the desk from me in military stockades and said, 'You know, sir, if the first time I had done something wrong they had clobbered me, I probably wouldn't be here now.' And I believe this remorseful hindsight on the part of these men is absolutely correct. I think it is harmful and unfair to the enlisted man to deprive him of a clear knowledge of the limits of permissible behavior and of the precise consequences of what will happen to him if he exceeds those limits. Under the present system, which vaguely seeks his cooperation and which for a long time demands little more, this essential clarity is all too often impossible."

I asked Brown whether he had any other ideas about increasing Army efficiency as a consequence of his work on the prisoner-of-war study, and he replied that he had. "Two other very important matters are closely tied to an increase of efficiency, and to the Army's potential ability to resist indoctrination," he told me. "The first is raising the level of the officer corps. We must get good officers and teach them above everything else they are leaders of men. Despite all the scientific advances, wars are still fought between men, simple, old-fashioned men; because of this, leadership is the inescapably vital factor. I wear an eagle on my shoulder, a major wears an oak leaf, a captain, bars . . . these are the trappings, the jewelry, of leadership. They should mean only one thing: that the wearer is a leader of men. Technicians and specialists, valuable as they are, should have different insignia and be attracted and held by devices other than leadership rank. These people—whose contributions are, of course, vital—should be rewarded on a different scale and be outwardly more differentiated than at present from men who are our combat leaders. Only in this way will we avoid confusion as to who and what our leaders are.

"Another help would be proper use of the fitness report. Too often a captain knows a lieutenant is lousy and says so in a fitness report, but the colonel turns it back because of sympathy, asking that it be made less harsh. Unless the captain wants to defy his superior and risk freezing his own career, he ups the report and the lieutenant goes on to promotion, a mediocre member of the Army, pulling the Army down. Supplementing proper use of the fitness report are ordinances, seldom invoked and, indeed, largely unknown, for getting rid of unfit, unqualified, or unmotivated personnel without a court-martial. For officers, it is Army Regulation Number 605-200. We don't like to be hard in the Army. But we should be, and must be. The argument that after a man's spent so many years in the service the Army owes him something is the vilest kind of bunk, and shouldn't be allowed to jeopardize the national security. If an officer can no longer pull his weight, he should be firmly separated. With better officers in our own ranks, and with the officer corps kept that way, there would be a natural tendency to swing back to the former Army system which closely paralleled the Canadian system. Our Canadian neighbors, for example, permit company-grade officers to deal summarily with practically all enlisted men's offenses by punishments that include fines up to one month's pay, reduction in rank, and imprisonments up to thirty days. And nobody in America thinks of the Canadians as beasts or as undemocratic. The whole experience in Korea showed how badly and desperately we need a return to the old Army system.

"A second thing that would help Army efficiency and render indoctrination more difficult, I feel, is to change the basis on which the Army is presented to recruits. The Army is in the unfortunate position of being a supplicant, trying unsuccessfully to sell itself to candidates on a material basis. Look at the Marines. They sell themselves—and they do a good job of it, too—on the basis of service, honor, and glory. What they say, in essence, is if you want to be a real, good man—if you want to join the best group of males in our society—then, buddy, be a Marine. And what happens? They get their men—the pick of the crop. But the Army tries misguidedly to sell itself on comfort. Pick your job, get security, join the U. S. Army, is its pitch. And it's a poor one. The implicit request is 'Please like us.'

"This is all wrong. Recruits and draftees should have to sell *themselves* to the Army, not the other way around. The tendency under the Doolittle influence is for the company commander to say to the newcomer, 'Joe, I'm the C.C. If there's anything I can do for you, please let me know.' Instead of truly leading men, we are trying to get them to come along with us on the basis of a popularity contest.

What seems to have been forgotten is that the Army is a fine, grand, proud organization, and that service in it is highly honorable and highly rewarding from the standpoint of spiritual and moral values. If people want security or a trade, these things are certainly widely obtainable in this country today. But these aren't the Army's business. Its appeal rests in honorable membership in the fraternity of fighting men on whom the country depends for its security. And the poorest way to prepare a man for any such duty, in my opinion, is to tell him where the snack bar is, what his rights and privileges under the Inspector General's system are, or try to make him feel instantly comfortable. I may sound overly hostile and unfriendly, but I know from dealing with hundreds of recruits that this is not the really kind or humanitarian approach. Young men coming into the Army naturally feel insecure; but the way to correct this is not to give them a false impression of comfort, tell them about the movie hour, and the time they will have off— or give them a company commander with the cooperative, democratic, let's-take-a-vote, and the please-come-along-now-fellows, and I-hope-you-will-like-me-fellows approach. The way to make a new man feel secure is for the Army to announce clearly and definitely what the limits of conduct are, and what it is going to require of him. And also, that while it's glad to have him presently in the ranks, he is strictly on probation and he'll have to improve a hell of a lot before he is competent to defend his country with a loaded rifle. I think we should go a little in the direction of telling

185

people coming into the Army that their responsibilities are now so enormous because the nation depends so heavily upon them, that we will have to make very severe demands upon them, indeed.

"Nobody pretends that the Army is going to be just heavenly and delightful. That's not what it's designed for. It's designed to protect the rest of society. Sold that way, I think the average American draftee will buy it more quickly and come out a better, more secure, more integrated, prouder soldier. And he will be well-disciplined. The well-disciplined kind of soldier probably won't get captured. But if he does—and there is no disgrace in it if his ammunition runs out, if he is wounded, or if he is overpowered —he will still be a proud, efficient American soldier in the prison camp. The enemy won't indoctrinate *him*, by God."

XVI

Early Army Remedial Moves

Containing Espionage—Survival Recommendations from Prison Doctors—Army Backing of Code of Conduct

Although the Army prisoner-of-war study discovered both praiseworthy and culpable acts performed by captives in Korea, unfortunately, for a number of complex reasons, the culpable acts predominated. These included, but did not end with, informing on fellow prisoners, writing or speaking propaganda for the enemy, helping through neglect to contribute to or cause the death of comrades, and accepting espionage missions.

The Army of course moved quickly to correct certain of these conditions. Espionage, it goes without saying, was one of the first to be counteracted. Adequate surveillance of suspects was the primary job, and the Army feels it early got control of the problem, which involved some seventy-five repatriates. "Keeping track of known, and also of potential, enemy agents is, of course, a two-fold task," Captain Cumby told me. "When they remain in the service, it's fairly easy. Once they leave it, the problem increases somewhat. We certainly can't, and we don't want to, keep every potentially disloyal civilian returnee under observation for the next ten years. But the whereabouts of some of them have to be known so that they can be watched. It's a matter, of course, that has been considered by the top-level security people in the Army; and definite plans have been made on how to deal with the problem.

"But perhaps even more important is the necessary contemplation of a future emergency. In any subsequent war with Communism," Cumby went on, "we must realize that the receipt of enemy-indoctrinated agents merely through the medium of prison exchange might assume such proportions that we could find ourselves threatened with a pretty important fifth column right in the midst of hostilities. Of course, there's nothing particularly new about this possibility—as a theory. But this much *is* new: because of the use of indoctrination by the Communists, the possibility of the situation occurring has definitely increased. This is another point for future consideration—to add to the already long list of things that the Army has learned from its experience in the Korean War."

Another step that the Army took as a result of the revelations of the prisoner-of-war study was action designed to cut down on prisoner death rates. To do this, the Army compiled a list of recommendations from doctors who had personally experienced Communist prison-camp treatment. Major Anderson told me that not long after repatriation he and four other Army physicians who had been captives were called in by the Surgeon General's Office in Washington to give their opinions on how Army personnel could be better prepared to survive the exigencies of life in a Communist prison camp. The doctors all agreed that by far the greatest error in our troop-training program had been to teach the men that Americans are "the best-cared-for soldiers on the globe."

"An American soldier goes into the field with comforts that the majority of the world's population doesn't have even at home," said Anderson. "He had been told that if he is wounded he will immediately be taken to a rear area and given adequate care. What our soldiers weren't told, however, was that if they were captured by the Communist enemy, all the comforts of life, which they take so much for granted, sick or well, would vanish into thin air. In Communist prison camps, such comforts simply do not exist. It should be explained emphatically to our soldiers that for centuries before this one, people got sick—and most of them subsequently got well—without extensive medication."

One of the first, most shocking things noted by all the doctors who had been in the prison camps, Anderson told me, was the reaction of the average prisoner to the lack of ordinary field and hospital comforts. He seemed lost without a bottle of pills and a toilet that flushed. In order to survive under prison conditions, a man must often eat things that would normally be repellent, such as wormy indigenous foods and dirty water; he must learn to live in filth, without proper sanitation, and not mind it too much. He must realize that he will die a lot sooner from starvation than he will from ailments that he might possibly contract by departing from the modes of sanitation to which he is accustomed.

"The prisoner in the Communist camp becomes an animal," said Anderson. "Plenty of people, including the Communists who were our enemies, live that way all their lives. If it means the difference between life and death, the policy of teaching our men also to live like animals for whatever time necessary should be adopted by us without hesitation or apology." In essence, the doctors who had been prisoners felt that the Army should continue to maintain the high standard of living of its soldiers in training and in the field; but at the same time it should make its trainees understand that if they were to be captured, those comforts might abruptly disappear, and should teach them how to get along with realistic and workable, if occasionally rigorous, substitutes.

The most important of all the steps that the Army took as a consequence of the discoveries of its prisoner-of-war study was to advocate a set of official conduct rules for the American fighting man. The Army felt strongly that these rules should state that an American taken prisoner be authorized to give to the enemy no information other than his name, rank, serial number, and date of birth. It felt that in the long run this policy would be best for the prisoner and best for his country, and that its prisoner-of-war study had showed this to be so. The Army's stand precipitated a lengthy controversy in the Pentagon. Without going into the details of the dispute, it can be said that the Air Force questioned the wisdom and practicality of the Army position, which was more or less supported by the other services. For months the services wrestled among themselves, until finally, nearly two years after the end of the Korean conflict, the problem was submitted to arbitration.

On May 18, 1955, Secretary of Defense Charles E. Wilson set up the Secretary of Defense's Advisory Committee on Prisoners of War to resolve the dispute. The committee's membership was composed of five civilians and five retired admirals and generals; retired officers were chosen because it was felt their judgments would be less partisan to any one particular service. The committee was headed by Carter L. Burgess, the Assistant Secretary of Defense for Manpower and Personnel; its vice-chairman was General John E. Hull, Army; and the other members were Dr. Frank Berry, Assistant Secretary of Defense for Health and Medicine; Hugh M. Milton II, Assistant Secretary of the Army for Manpower and Reserve Forces; Albert Pratt, Assistant Secretary of the Navy for Personnel and Reserve Forces; David S. Smith, Assistant Secretary of the Air Force for Manpower and Personnel; Lieutenant General Frank W.

Milburn, Army; Vice-Admiral C. A. Lockwood, Navy; Lieutenant General Idwal H. Edwards, Air Force; and Major General Merritt A. Edson, Marine Corps.

The Army argued its position vigorously to the committee, stating that from practical, psychological, and moral viewpoints its stand was right. One spokesman for the Army viewpoint, Colonel Perry, put it this way:

"As far as the practicality of the Army point of view is concerned," Colonel Perry said to me, "it's only when a prisoner gives more than his name, rank, serial number, and date of birth that he gets into trouble. If he tries to argue ideology with an interrogator and to point out flaws in the Communist philosophy, he is attempting what many of our highly trained diplomats have been unsuccessful at. If he decides to take it upon himself to determine what is unimportant military information, he is trifling with the lives of his comrades in the line. Captured documents offer many examples of prisoners giving information they thought was unimportant, which profited the enemy enormously. Even answering so apparently innocuous a query as 'Where did you get on the truck?' gave the Chinese, who were largely air-blind in the Korean War, a vital clue to a hitherto unknown troop-assembly point.

"There is a third way of countering enemy questions," continued Colonel Perry, "no better than these other two, which is to give false answers. Prisoners have resorted to falsehood in every war in history, and the military intelligence systems of every army have sure ways to detect it.

The most experienced officers have tried it without success, so it would be folly to urge the average prisoner to do so." In addition, the Colonel said, when men tried to lie to the Chinese Communists, they faced a hitherto unheard-of and very serious disadvantage. Under the Communists' exceedingly stringent disciplinary code, a lie may be treated —out of all proportion to Western standards—as a penal offense, punishable, as it often is punished in China today, by death. The few cases in the Army study in which physical torture or death was inflicted on prisoners by the Communists were cases in which the prisoners had not resisted interrogation or indoctrination, but had lied or committed other infringements of Chinese civil or military law. "The Army has no hesitation in saying that a prisoner should stick firmly and honestly to the name, number, date-of-birth line. In the long run, as was proved in Korea, it's his best protection," said Perry.

A widely-held theory advanced to the committee during its deliberations by opponents of the Army's view was that it was possible for prisoners to go part way with Communist captors. The Army disagreed with this presumption, citing in rebuttal those of its captives who had played it cool, or yielded without doing anything that was obviously traitorous. These men believed that the Communists would be more lenient with those who did not resist them, but this belief was completely wrong, as time proved. Many repatriates, in their discussions of enemy interrogation sessions, told operatives of our Joint Intelligence Processing Teams,

"There never was any point to yielding. If I'd known what it would have meant eventually, I never would have given in the first time." The Communists were never more lenient with or less demanding of those prisoners who did not resist them; actually, the opposite was true.

Major Segal, the psychiatrist, outlined for me the psychological reasons behind the behavior of those who played it cool. "The psychological motive behind so much of what these men did was their erroneous anticipation of what might happen to them if they didn't do it. If I don't sign this, I will be tortured, they thought, and, in psychiatric interviews, told us that this was what they thought. If only it could have been pointed out to this group that their attitude was not realistic, and if they could then have based their behavior on what was real, rather than on what was fantasy, the entire camp experience could have been easier for all of them. The main trouble with these men's playing it cool was that their compliance was actually what made the Communists' system operate. Without it, the Communists would have been powerless."

Segal added his support, on psychological grounds, to the effectiveness of silence as a countermeasure. "Talking is always the first step toward collaborating," he told me. "Once a man starts talking, there is no escape from more talking. And the more he talks, the greater his guilt and anxiety. These have very important psychological results. His guilt and anxiety absorb a lot of his psychic energy, which makes him less able to cope with the normal stresses and strains of prison life. His whole personality tends to disintegrate. He knows he has done something wrong by submitting to the Communist demands, and his conscience will not let him rest. The 'mental torture' offered as an excuse for their conduct by certain collaborators who have been tried in court was not necessarily something inflicted by the Communists. It could in most cases more accurately have been termed self-torture. Certainly every psychiatrist saw ample signs of this guilt and anxiety in the repatriates they interviewed on the voyage home.

"If I knew any future GI who was slated to be captured by the Communists," Segal continued, "I would say to him, 'First, you must know that your own best chance for survival lies in your not talking. And, second, you must know that your *buddies*' best chance for survival also lies in your not talking.' I would see that the man was packed full of arguments on why he must not talk. A good part of these would be examples from case histories of men who *had* talked. If a man doesn't talk, he can't incriminate himself. Or anybody else. Or give information. Or be duped. The best way to maintain silence, and loyalty, I would tell him, is by joining with other soldiers to keep discipline and help each other. Survival is an absolute impossibility for one man without the support of the group, and the way a man behaves is, to a large degree, dependent on how the group permits him to behave. When *esprit de corps* and discipline are preserved, men are brave and resistant; and the opposite is unalterably true. This is elementary, but in the

195

Korean War some men seemed to forget it. Once a man abandons silence and starts talking, the picture is black. He has to keep asking himself constantly, 'What did I say? Is my story still straight? Did I implicate So-and-So? Should I confess to this false crime? If I do, will my buddies understand? If I do, will I become a criminal?' and yet a man *can't* stop talking if he once starts. Once having yielded to pressure, he is more vulnerable than ever, psychologically, to future pressures. Invariably he goes on."

The Army felt that it was on sound moral ground when it asked that its men taken captive abide by its traditions and by the rules of the Geneva Convention, reserving at the same time, as it deemed proper, the right to prosecute those who had violated the laws of the Uniform Code of Military Justice. "In the confused disciplinary climate caused by problems created in the Korean War," Colonel Trammell told me, "this stand by the Army—which meant that whoever yielded to the enemy's indoctrination and interrogation ran the risk of being tried—was criticized by many as being too puritanical and unrealistic. Before the matter was resolved by the Code of Conduct, the critics included certain members within the armed services themselves. One highly placed naval officer for instance, acting not officially but as an informed individual, published an article in *The Saturday Evening Post* in which he said that the most logical and effective answer to indoctrination and interrogation would be a campaign of mass lying by our men. This seemed like a very simple and easy solution, and it received enthusiastic support in many quarters. The idea was that our men should say, with later impunity, anything that the Communists wanted them to say, drawing on their imaginations, if they wished, to elaborate their statements in order to make them seem absurd to the outside world. The theory was that this sort of compliant mendacity would not expose the prisoner to the risk of Communist punishment; and such obvious widespread and exaggerated falsehood would nullify the enemy program."

Trammell explained that the reason that the Army did not support this idea was simple. "The Army," he said, "felt that one of the prime objectives of Communism is to destroy the moral fabric of America, which is our basic strength. To allow, much less to encourage, our soldiers to lie, to cheat, and to deceive would be merely to permit the Communists to gain this objective without even having to try, and to undermine one of the most powerful assets that this nation possesses—its love of truth." Trammell pointed out that this love of truth and our identification with it have vast practical as well as vast spiritual values. "Our devotion to truth has given us world leadership and world respect," he said. "As an example, after the armistice when we offered to provide asylum for any Communist prisoner who wished to remain on our side of the line, a flattering total of more than 23,000 accepted. These men had been taught in our prison camp what democracy stands for, and they liked and believed what they heard. They included 15,000 out of the 22,000 Chinese captured, or a ratio of two in three of the fighting men of the more formidable enemy force that were taken in that war. The Chinese who came with us knew that they could not immediately, or perhaps ever, return to their homeland. Nevertheless, they made their decision, conscious that in joining with us they were joining with the side that supported truth. Their belief in us and their faith in us—and the belief and faith in us of every hopeless and enslaved person around the world—is a position of practical power that immeasurably enhances our international status. It would be impossible, the Army believed, to maintain that status if our official policy were to deceive."

The Secretary of Defense's Advisory Committee on Prisoners of War reviewed impartially all prisoner-of-war problems that had arisen in Korea. During an intensive three-month survey it questioned nearly seventy civilians and members of all four of the armed forces who had either special or first-hand knowledge of Korean prisoner problems, and it examined scores of documents and papers bearing on the subject.

For the first month or so, General John E. Hull, the vice-chairman of the committee, told me, the members did little talking among themselves. "They listened, instead, quite intently to the testimony," he said. "Nobody knew exactly how the other fellow felt. Nobody, at first, was inclined to express his views. Then gradually, bit by bit, the committee members opened up. 'Well, it looks to me like this,' one of them would say at last. And the odd thing was that when everybody had spoken, we found we all thought alike. And yet maybe, on second thought, it isn't so odd. Any American, I guess, who goes into this matter seriously will come up with just about the same answer. We all agreed that there might be exceptions to our thinking based on circumstances for which no rule could be given beforehand, but we also all agreed that American servicemen in the future must realize they are responsible for their acts.

"One thing in particular we were anxious to do," General Hull went on, "and that was to protect a man to the maximum from getting himself in a jam. Soviet Russia and most of the Communist states had agreed to the 1949 Geneva Convention with certain reservations; one of the reservations has the effect of making a prisoner a 'war criminal' in Communist eyes if he signs or makes certain statements which the detaining power could construe as a confession of guilt for any crime that under its laws could be considered a war crime, such as a confession of using germ warfare. For their own protection, therefore, the committee felt that military personnel should be trained to say no more than they have to in any effort to hold their own in a battle of wits with enemy interrogators. The committee felt that a line of resistance should be drawn somewhere, and initially as far forward as possible. The name, rank, service number, and date-of-birth provision of the Geneva Conference was accepted as this line of resistance. In advocating this, the committee thought it was accomplishing two things: it was meeting the military needs of the country, and it was doing this in a manner compatible with the principles and precepts of our form of government."

In August, 1955, the President promulgated the Code of Conduct which the committee recommended. Essentially, it supported the findings of the Army prisoner-of-war study.

XVII

The Army and
the Code

Later Army Remedial Moves—Some Sixty Directives, Films, and
Pamphlets Now Support or Illuminate Code—Army's Appeal to
Citizens to Consider Its Study

After the Code of Conduct became a fact, the Army and
the other branches of the country's armed forces issued
regulations and instructions to support it, each service acting in the way it thought best to implement the new rules.
In the nearly thirty months since the Code's promulgation,
the Army has produced approximately sixty directives, films,
or pamphlets completely or partly concerned with the
Code's fulfillment.

The Army training program seeks to meet the Communist challenge in two broad areas of activity—in combat
and in captivity. "Although most of the trouble in Korea
came from prison-camp activities," an instructional expert

at Camp Benning, an Army post in Georgia, told me, "don't for a moment suppose we are primarily teaching our GI's how to be prisoners of war. The essential purpose of our training—and the essential purpose of the Code—is to teach young Americans how to be better fighting men, healthy, hardy, well-disciplined, and properly motivated soldiers who will not only stay out of enemy hands, but will force the enemy into ours."

To achieve the efficiency it seeks, the Army has put greater emphasis upon leadership in its training. "We must have leadership with initiative," this spokesman said. "We must produce good officers—commissioned and noncommissioned—and teach them that above all else they are leaders of men. In our leadership reaction courses, we stress situations where an on-the-spot solution is required under the most difficult conditions we can contrive. We are ordering continual and sustained combat training at stations all over the world, picking difficult terrain and operating regardless of weather—in deserts, swamps, and mountains, during snow and rain and particularly at night. Our men must have initiative and sound leadership. An army can have physical and technical perfection, but without initiative and sound leadership, everything else goes down the drain."

The Army has also instituted a replacement policy known as *Operation Gyroscope*. Under it, units instead of individuals are rotated in assignments at home and abroad. This, it is believed, will enable a soldier to identify more strongly with those men immediately around him, and, as a result, greatly increase his loyalty to them. The unit should thus be more effective in combat, and, if any of its members are captured, they should, through this group solidarity, be more able—as were the Turks and Marines—to resist pressure in a prison camp.

As a result of its experience in Korea, the Army has dramatically changed its policy about telling men what to do in case of capture. This, too, is reflected in the Code training. In the past, it was felt that if a man were given detailed information on how to act in a prison camp, he might be more likely to surrender. But Korea—and the changing nature of war in general—have, the Army thinks, made this argument outmoded. The greater mobility of troops in combat and the use of paratroopers increase the risk of capture. The old argument, it is now felt, is like saying that a sailor should be forbidden to learn to swim because his superiors want him to stay with his ship until the last possible moment. But what happens if, in spite of all his determination, an enemy torpedo dumps him into the water and he finds himself six feet from a life preserver? Figuratively speaking, this occurred too many times in Korean prison camps. The Army now realizes that a man's prior knowledge of a situation in which he could be placed may eventually be absolutely necessary for his survival; and the Army's training program now provides men with this information. For example, it has introduced evasion and escape maneuvers in which small bodies of troops are cut off from their units and try to work their way back to their own lines through superior numbers of "aggressors." If captured, they are subjected to treatment, which, although not as severe as the real thing, approximates Communist handling.

As usual in such matters, the Army does not have the wholehearted cooperation of all trainees. Recently it received a letter from a Congressman protesting the rigors of post-Korean instruction. The Congressman complained that a constituent had been harshly questioned and forced to strip to the waist in a temperature of thirty-five degrees Fahrenheit and run about a simulated prisoner compound. On investigation, the Army found the soldier had received this mildly realistic treatment in its evasion and escape course. In its response to the Congressman, the Army observed that in view of the current international situation such training "is not considered extreme, but vital, fruitful, and necessary."

Despite the scope of its program, which it intends to enlarge as necessary, the Army realizes there is much work to be done in getting proper information about the Code to its troops. A study testing the effectiveness of instruction, made eighteen months after the Code was promulgated, showed serious flaws. The survey was taken among more than three thousand Army personnel stationed in this country and overseas. The most important error it revealed was that 10 per cent of those taking the test believed that the Code permitted a prisoner to broadcast enemy propaganda appeals.

Army training devices approach the problem of Code training from a number of angles. Many stress positive action as a soldier: "Your job in the Army is to be able to do your duty when called upon. Regardless of your branch of service or job assignment, your ultimate goal *is to be prepared* to fight" (from the directive, *Combat Training*). Others have broad educational aims: "Prejudice *hurts*. In the first place, it is Contagious. The bias we have against one group today may be used against another tomorrow" (from the pamphlet, *Duty, Honor, Country*). The purpose of all the devices is to make our troops better Americans and thus, among other things, better able to resist Communist blandishments should they land in a prison camp.

Some of these aids require an instructor, while others can be assimilated individually. Here is part of the script of a ten-minute film illustrating Article V of the Code, which states that a prisoner when questioned is bound to give only his name, rank, service number, and date of birth:

It is six o'clock by an old-fashioned wall clock in an almost completely dark room. Luminous hands tell the time. The tick is heard distinctly when the Camera is on the clock—hold for few seconds.

Enemy Interrogator's Voice (angry—good English with accent): "I've never lost a man yet—I've never failed to obtain my objective."

Enemy interrogator is backlit by spotlight behind each shoulder trained on the American POW across the table. The interrogator seems more terrifying because his face is so indistinct. He's something out of a nightmare. End of guard's tommy gun is included in shot.

Interrogator: "And I've had them tougher than you—admit the name of your battle group commander was Colonel Perry—your Company Commander Captain Logan—(*Waits—bangs fist on table*)—Answer me!"

POW's Voice (*steady tone*): "Banks, Paul J.—Corporal—Service Number 39024008—born 15 August 1956."

Interrogator: "Stupid!—too stupid to know you're just another running dog for Wall Street—you're a dog and I'm going to treat you like a dog—strip off everything—(*While he waits he lights a cigarette; the lighter reveals evilly angry eyes; lighter goes out*). Why are you shivering?—it's 31 degrees Fahrenheit in here—are you shivering because you finally have sense enough to be afraid? Here you only make us laugh with your Geneva Conference rules and your Code of Conduct. Your outfit is the 34th Airborne Infantry—answer, you dog!"

Banks, seated, shivering. He's plenty scared but hiding it. He remains silent.

Interrogator's Voice: "Do you know how we torture people? (*Banks manages to maintain a deadpan.*) One way is to lash a copper bowl upside down on your naked stomach—underneath the bowl are large rats, hungry to the point of starvation. The rats proceed to eat their way out of captivity through your stomach."

And the going gets even grimmer, but the prisoner holds out. The hands on the clock point to nine. The scene continues.

Interrogator leans across the table waving paper and pen.

Interrogator: "Sign this document admitting it. This is your last chance—(*He waits—silence.*) Take your clothes and get out of here, dog. I have no more time for you now. You'll see me again soon. (*Gestures to guard to take Banks away.*) And if you still can't use your tongue, I'll cut it off."

So silence wins, just as it did in Korea. No one can see the film without identifying with the prisoner—feeling the cold and the dark, shaking when he shakes, holding out when he holds out. It is second only to the actual experience of resisting an interrogator.

The Army is doing nothing officially, I learned, to incorporate into its present training program the views of Colonel Brown, who seeks stiffer discipline and greater latitude for the company commander despite the fact that these views are supported by the records of the Marines and the Turks, the two control groups who were held prisoner under the same conditions as Army men in Korea. Brown has support for his beliefs within the service, but another group feels that all necessary discipline can be enforced under current regulations. How the debate will be eventually resolved seems, at the moment, anybody's guess.

"By now you have a broad picture of the conditions among Korean prisoners that were revealed by the Army's prisoner-of-war study," said Mr. Milton when I saw him for the last time. "And you know something about what caused these conditions, and why it was necessary to set up the Code of Conduct. As you realize, the picture isn't a completely pretty one, or one of which we are uniformly proud. But it has its compensations. For one thing, the Army has now met a Communist enemy for the first time, and as a result we have a good insight into Communist methods for handling prisoners. They play no favorites, we have learned. What they did to us, they do to their own

people. Now that we know what they do, we've found that
the Army's training and previous standards of conduct,
while essentially right, did not go far enough toward teaching a prisoner what he could expect in Communist hands.
We have, therefore, taken additional steps to prepare the
men for what was encountered in Korea, and we are con-
fident that these steps will be helpful. I ought to say at this
point, too, that when we learned more about Communist
prisoner-handling methods and began to understand them,
we were happy so many of our men had stood up so well
under the circumstances when they had nothing to fall back
on but their own staunch characters and our insufficient
training.

"Experience has shown that the Communists are a
heartless enemy who will humiliate and debase those in
their hands for their own purposes," Milton continued.
"The soldier's best defense against this treatment, of course,
is his own raw courage. But the Army now realizes that a
man's nerve can be greatly stiffened by teaching him exactly
how his captors will go about breaking that nerve. Their
step-by-step undermining of loyalty will be made much
more difficult if our troops are forewarned. Returned prisoners have agreed that one of the best possible defenses
against Communist tactics would be *mental preparation*
for them. That sounds elementary; and yet it is a new concept resulting from a new set of international conditions and
the new experiences we had in Korea. Our men may be
deprived of sleep, food, and medical attention in a prison

camp. They should expect this and still have the will to live while these things are temporarily lacking. They should also acquire a familiarity with first aid, nutrition, and preventive medicine—all substantial helps under such conditions. On the spiritual side, *esprit de corps* and a feeling of comradeship are great aids to morale. So are a faith in democracy and an adherence to religious beliefs. Many repatriates told us that in the prison camps religious and ethical intangibles were of greater help and comfort to them than anything else. Now, even more than in the past, they will bulk large in Army training."

One of the more important of the new Army regulations is one establishing a complete and detailed code of conduct for troops after capture, based on the general six-point Code of Conduct, Milton told me. "Many men who collaborated in prison camps," he said, "pleaded innocent of misconduct because they said they acted on orders from their superiors. One of the hardest things to make clear, legally and logically, is that a man has a loyalty to discipline, but also an independent loyalty to his country. The two should be reconciled, and they must be reconciled if our men are to cope with as devious an enemy as the Communists, who, of course, plan and hope that orders favorable to their own ends will be issued by weak officers and that weak men will obey them. In the new regulation, the Army feels that these two kinds of loyalty have been reconciled."

Article V of the Code of Conduct has a sentence concerning interrogation which reads "I will evade answering further questions to the best of my ability." The Army nevertheless intends to adhere to its policy of authorizing the prisoner to give the enemy nothing more than his name, rank, serial number, and date of birth. The reason for this, the Army says, is simple. Its study showed that men were not tortured and did not die as a result of their refusal to give more information than this. The study also showed that every man whose court-martial was authorized by the Army began his record of misconduct by talking too much; that is, by offering information beyond these basic facts. The Army's decision to hold to this line was reached after months of investigation and discussion about the best course to follow—practically as well as ethically. "You can argue about such things till doomsday, but the Communist challenge has got to be met," said Milton. "And it's got to be met in an American way—no compromise with evil. If this means our troops must withstand emotional pressure and psychological pain in order to uphold standards sanctioned throughout the civilized world, then, for the good of the country, these must be borne. If the Communists alter their methods to include physical torture, this must be endured, too. Any deviation from this, in the Army's opinion, would only delay our ultimate victory."

The Army, Milton went on, wants as many people as possible to think about these matters. "Overcoming Communism is not simply an Army problem," he said. "It's a truly national problem. And don't forget—the battle against Communism is waged largely at the level of the individual, and the earlier he is prepared, the better. The Army would like to see every American parent, every American teacher, and every American clergyman work to instill in every one of our children a specific understanding of the differences between our way of life and the Communist way of life, and, even more important, work to give every child, in the blunt, old-fashioned spirit, a firm regard for right and an abiding distaste for wrong. The Army's period of training is too brief to make changes in the habits of a lifetime. By the time a young man enters the Army, he should possess a set of sound moral values and the strength of character to live by them. Then, with Army training, he may become something very close to military perfection—the ideal citizen soldier."

Index

213